Sarah Ockwell-Smith is the mother of four children. She has a BSc in Psychology and worked for several years in pharmaceutical research and development. Following the birth of her first child, Sarah retrained as an antenatal teacher and birth and postnatal doula. She has also undertaken training in hypnotherapy and psychotherapy.

Sarah specialises in gentle parenting methods and is the author of eleven other parenting books: *BabyCalm*, *ToddlerCalm*, *The Gentle Sleep Book*, *The Gentle Parenting Book*, *Why Your Baby's Sleep Matters*, *The Gentle Discipline Book*, *The Gentle Potty Training Book*, *The Gentle Eating Book*, *The Second Baby Book*, *The Starting School Book* and *Between*. She frequently writes for magazines and newspapers, and is often called upon as a parenting expert for national television and radio. Sarah also blogs at www.sarahockwell-smith.com.

SARAH OCKWELL-SMITH

HOW TO BE A CALM PARENT

Lose the guilt, control your anger
and **tame the stress** – for more
peaceful and enjoyable parenting
and calmer, happier children too

PIATKUS

PIATKUS

First published in Great Britain in 2022 by Piatkus

1 3 5 7 9 10 8 6 4 2

Copyright © Sarah Ockwell-Smith 2022
The moral right of the author has been asserted.

A CIP catalogue record for this book
is available from the British Library.

ISBN 978-0-349-43126-0

Illustrations © Louise Turpin
Typeset in Stone Serif by M Rules
Printed and bound in Great Britain by
Clays Ltd, Elcograf S.p.A

Papers used by Piatkus are from well-managed forests
and other responsible sources.

MIX
Paper from
responsible sources
FSC® C104740

Piatkus
An imprint of
Little, Brown Book Group
Carmelite House
50 Victoria Embankment
London EC4Y 0DZ

An Hachette UK Company
www.hachette.co.uk

www.littlebrown.co.uk

Contents

Introduction   1

Chapter 1
Shadows from the nursery – understanding
your triggers and making peace with
your own childhood   11

Chapter 2
The quest for parenting perfection – embrace
your own failures and rid yourself of guilt   43

Chapter 3
The curse of comparison – and why it hinders
and deceives us   61

Chapter 4
The mental and physical load of parenting –
and why we must get better at sharing it   75

Chapter 5
Moving with the tide and letting go of control –
how to tackle life transitions with grace   100

Chapter 6
Why busy is not a badge to aim for – discovering
the lost art of doing nothing   117

Chapter 7
Relationships with partners, other parents and
wider family – and why these impact your
relationship with your child   132

Chapter 8
 Balancing work and home life – why we must
stop aiming to 'have it all'   157

Chapter 9
The importance of self-kindness – introducing
the Peaceful Pentagon   173

Chapter 10
Taming the storm and coping in the moment
(AKA how to not throw your own tantrums
and what to do if you do)   199

Chapter 11
The seven golden rules of calmer parenting –
a refresher and a closing note   220

References   227
Resources   233
Index   235

Introduction

This isn't a parenting book. It's a book about you. However, the words you read here will have a far greater impact on your children than those contained in any parenting book you could read (and I count my own, too).

This book has been brewing in the back of my mind for at least ten years, but I didn't feel I could do it justice until now. Why? Because, although I'm a so-called 'parenting expert', I was not a calm parent. I struggled hugely with anger outbursts and yelling. I yelled a lot. I was a major stress-head. I have also been prone to experiencing crippling feelings of inadequacy and guilt, with a good side order of anxiety thrown in. I'm not perfect or uber-zen now (anybody who tells you they are is lying), but I've managed to do a lot of work on myself over the last couple of years and now I finally feel qualified to tell you all about it. I may not be the calmest parent out there, but I'm proud of what I've achieved, and I know that you can achieve so much, too.

My own journey to calmer parenting started in earnest in the autumn of 2019 when I was diagnosed with cancer. Until then I had dabbled in self-care, tried yoga and Pilates classes, listened to guided meditations and practised mindfulness when I could, but if I'm honest, my efforts were all a little half-hearted. Frankly, I was just too busy – ironically, writing parenting advice books and coaching other parents – to invest the time and effort necessary to truly honour my own needs. My cancer diagnosis floored me. I was too busy to be ill. I fought against my mind and my body, my doctors and my friends and family, too, as I tried to carry on as I had been, pushing the cancer to the back of my mind, focusing on everybody else's needs and not my own. I was back at work the day after major surgery and carried on professionally as if nothing was any different.

My saving grace came, unbelievably, in the form of the Covid-19 pandemic. Lockdown arrived just as I was starting to recuperate from my treatment. I was forced to stay at home and confront my demons. I had no choice but to relax and to spend a lot more time alone with my thoughts. I couldn't hide in my busyness or my business, any more. I had to face the fact that the way I had been living was not healthy or sustainable for me or my family. The heavy burden of stress, anger and unresolved feelings was delaying my recovery. I had to change for me. My previous – unsuccessful – attempts to be more composed had been solely about my children, but now they could literally save my life. This was deeply personal now. I had more fire than ever before to change and become calmer.

Now, as trite as it sounds, I view my cancer as a gift. I am grateful for the lessons it taught me and for the metamorphosis it triggered. It woke me up to the true value of life and how we all deserve to feel happy and calm. We deserve to enjoy, not just survive, parenting. I can genuinely say that I am emotionally at the best point I have ever been at now – something a lot of people struggle to understand given what I went through. This is not an uncommon feeling among cancer survivors I have learned, though. I now refer to my life as BC (before cancer) and AC (after cancer). The AC me is totally different to the BC me when it comes to coping with my emotions. In fact, over the last year, many people have commented on how calm I am, given the circumstances.

The change didn't happen overnight, though. I worked hard to recognise and, ultimately, heal my issues and I'm still a work in progress. I know I have more work to do, but now I approach life with a level of peace and calm that I never had before. In this book, I am going to share the steps and processes that led me to become calmer, happier and more peaceful – not just with my children, but with myself, too.

Until recently, I made the mistake of reading every single negative review for my books online. Later in this book I'm going to tell you to avoid activities that you know will torment you, one of the things I've been working on a lot myself. I'm glad I didn't take my own advice in my BC days, though, because one of the negative reviews I read proved really valuable. Somebody had left a one-star review for my *Gentle Discipline Book*, that read: 'I felt like the premise was basically – if you have your crap together, so will your kids.' I sat and stared at the screen, totally bemused, for several minutes. That absolutely *was* the premise of the book, and I made no attempt to hide it. In fact, it's pretty much the underlying premise of *all* my books. I would even go so far as to say that every decent parenting book that's ever been written is really about what the parents do, not the children. Great parenting isn't about what you say to your kids, or any magic techniques you may employ with them – it's about who you are and how you tackle your own demons to ensure you don't pass them on to your children. The irony of that one-star review that totally encapsulated the absolute best parenting advice wasn't lost on me, and it sparked an idea that eventually became this book. Although I've written plenty of parenting books, what I have never done, until now, that is, is to write a book to tell parents exactly *how* to 'have their crap together'.

I did wonder if I should include some information in this introduction about why parents should be calmer, why shouting is bad for children and why we all need to work to be less stressed, less anxious and less angry. I'm not so sure this sort of information really helps anybody, though. While there are plenty of research studies I could quote here to support this position, I don't think we need to read them. We all *know*, deep down, that losing our cool with our children isn't good for them. We all *know* that our lack of emotional regulation at times is potentially harmful to our children. We've all felt those pangs of shame and regret when we didn't hold it together and lost control at, or around, our children. We all *know* how it feels to be a child on the receiving end of an out-of-control parent or carer yelling at us. We all *know* that the best home a child could grow in is one with a calm, emotionally stable and secure parent, or parents. I don't want to add to your guilt any more. I think you've probably punished yourself enough. You're already reading this book, you already know you need to change and, most importantly, you *want* to change. I think that's more than enough!

Who is this book for?

The short answer? Everyone!

The long answer? Everyone who has children, is thinking of having children or works with children. It doesn't matter how old the children are, how old you are, how many children you have or care for, and it doesn't matter what gender you are, whether you spend all day at home with children or work away from them all week. If you are an adult who spends some time with children, who recognises the need to be calmer, both with the children and away from them, then this book is for you.

The seven golden rules of calmer parenting

The older I've become, the less keen I am on the use of rules, but I think it's important to set the scene and simplify a little here. Throughout this book I will discuss many things that impact on our state of mind and actions as parents. I think it's important to take a holistic view and to ask *why* we struggle to be calm before we even begin to think about what we can do to be calmer. The answer to the 'why am I like this?' question is anything but simple and straightforward. I do, however, believe that a few simple guidelines to start with make the process to becoming calm easier. Hence my top seven rules:

1. **Everybody can be a calmer parent.** It doesn't take any special personality traits. Privilege does inevitably mean that life is infinitely easier for some, but we can *all* do some work and make some changes that will have a positive impact, regardless of our life situation (although I do accept that lack of privilege can – and will – limit what's possible).

2. **Everybody loses it at times.** Nobody is calm 100 per cent of the time – nobody should aim to be. We must lower the bar when it comes to expectations of what we can achieve, and we must not compare our 'inner selves' (our innermost thoughts and feelings) with the 'outer selves' (the carefully curated illusion) of others. You are not alone. All parents act in ways they're ashamed of. Everybody has to try hard to hold it together. Losing your temper doesn't mean you're not good enough or are lacking willpower and it definitely does not make you a worse parent than somebody else.

3. **It is not your fault that you aren't a calm parent.** Read that again and stop blaming yourself. Parents carry such a burden of guilt and instantly blame themselves when they get angry and short-tempered with their children. But it isn't your fault. We are who we are due to the way we were raised, the situations we find ourselves in and the relationships we have with others. Don't think 'what's wrong with me?' Instead, see yourself as a combination of things that have happened to you and the environment you are in – you are not flawed. And the good news is you can assert some control over how you process these experiences and the hold they have on you in the future.

4. **You are still going to have lots of big feelings.** You are not aiming to get rid of the big feelings, just to cope with them in a healthier way. You will still feel anger, frustration, worry and disappointment, in both yourself and your children. And that's OK. All feelings are OK. In short, the key to being calmer is allowing and accepting these big feelings and turning reactivity into responsivity: putting a space between your child's actions, your feelings and your response. Becoming calmer is about self-awareness, self-acceptance and self-forgiveness, not trying to turn yourself into some sort of emotionally devoid robot.

5. **Messing up doesn't undo all the good you've done before.** A bad day is simply that – a bad day. It does not make you a bad person or a failure. Even if that day stretches into weeks, months or years. It doesn't undo the work you have previously put in to becoming calmer or cancel out the good days. It also doesn't have any impact on what you can achieve in the future. The road to calmer parenting is full of ups and downs. You will mess up, you will feel like you've taken a million steps back

some days, but you just need to keep going and accept the topsy-turvy route to progress. Real life is messy and so is real change.

6. **The journey to becoming calmer takes time**. Make sure your goals are realistic. You're not going to change overnight, or even in a month or two. You are going to be a work in progress for pretty much the rest of your life, and that's OK – because even a tiny change is still a change. Although it may sound terribly clichéd, a thousand tiny steps will get you further than one giant leap. Commitment and consistency are key; repeated small changes are better than one-off attempts at enormous change.

7. **You will not screw up your child when you 'lose it'.** This is maybe the most important rule to really and truly assimilate because the guilt we carry with us when we screw up can have such a damaging effect on our future attempts. Children are resilient, and our mistakes as parents help them to grow. What matters more is how you heal any rift that happens afterwards. Later, I will talk about the 'rupture-and-repair' cycle, or as I prefer to call it 'holler and heal'. Knowing how to heal any hurt caused during our inevitable 'uncalm' moments is part of the foundation of calmer parenting. So too is learning to palliate any feelings of inadequacy and guilt that accompany them, to turn them into something productive instead.

How to use this book

The process of becoming a calmer parent is rather like a huge jigsaw puzzle, with many pieces. If the puzzle is incomplete, because there is an aspect you haven't considered or worked on, then the final picture – and result – will be lacking. With this in mind, I recommend that you read all the chapters in this book, even if they don't all automatically speak to you, and I'd advise focusing on one at a time to allow you to fully absorb the messages and work on any exercises and changes. Of course, it's OK to read the book straight through in a few days, but I'd advise then going back and picking a chapter to really work on, on a deeper level. The order you do this in, however, is less important, so feel free to dip in and out, starting with those chapters you find most pertinent to you. Having said that, Chapter 1 should be everybody's starting point. To look forwards and make changes to your parenting, you must begin with some reflection on your own childhood. Chapter 1 discusses the shadows from your upbringing (we all have them, no matter how wonderful our parents are, or were). This helps to identify and understand your biggest triggers, and allows you to make any necessary peace with the way in which you were raised, so that you can leave unhelpful generational patterns firmly where they belong, in the past.

In Chapter 2, we will talk about the alarming quest for parenting perfection that seems so pertinent in our age of oversharing. We will consider why it's so important to embrace our own authentic parenting style and to remove the guilt that is not only unhelpful, but incredibly toxic. Chapter 3 continues the theme of perceived parenting perfection and discusses how the tendency to constantly compare our parenting ability to that of others can be toxic and damage our ability to be a calm parent. In Chapter 4, we look at one aspect of parenting that can weigh us down and lead to exhaustion, which is sure to negatively impact our state of mind, as well as our physical stamina. The so-called 'mental load of parenting' may be a relatively new concept in terms of awareness and discussion, but its roots run deep. Hopefully, we can be the generation not only to raise awareness, but also to make a change towards some much-needed equality.

Chapter 5 focuses on transitions and big life changes, which can – and do – impact on our state of mind and emotional control. I talk about the idea of moving with the tide, rather than fighting the waves, and learning to let go of some control – something we could probably all do a little more. Moving on to Chapter 6, the focus shifts to the modern notion of the busy parent and how juggling many balls successfully seems to be seen by many as a badge of honour and a mark of respect. These beliefs, however, are misguided. Instead, I argue for the lost art of doing nothing, and why less is so much more when it comes to our parenting mindset and emotional health.

In Chapter 7, our attention turns to our external relationships, having focused so far on our relationships with ourselves. We will consider the interactions and exchanges we have with our partners, or ex-partners in the case of co-parenting, friends and wider family and why these adult relationships impact that with your child. We will look at the connections you have with other adults and how they play an important role in your parenting, not only for the better, but sometimes to its detriment – which is why we also discuss how to let go of those friends and connections if they're not positive for you.

Chapter 8 covers that all-important balance between work and home life and why we must stop aiming to 'have it all'. Indeed, the art of balance means a constant shift in the weight of each part, gently removing a little of one and adding a little more of the other, until equilibrium is reached. In Chapter 9, I introduce my idea of 'the Peaceful Pentagon', five essential points that keep us healthy in body and mind – the concepts of eating well, sleeping well, moving well, resting well and spending time in nature, with all its healing properties. I will also discuss why I don't believe the current focus of society on 'self-care' practices for parents is a useful or helpful one. The path to calmer parenting is not paved by bubble baths and massages. Instead, I focus on 'self-kindness': putting your own needs at the heart of your actions, without the pressure to behave or act in a certain way.

Chapter 10 – which, after Chapter 1, I believe is the second most important – talks about what to do when you lose your cool. It is unrealistic to aim for being calm all the time. Regardless of the amount of work you put in and how much you embrace the concepts introduced in Chapters 1 through 9, you *will* lose your cool and act in a way that you are not proud of towards your child. This is inevitable. Here, what you need are tips to cope with the aftermath, how to holler and then heal. How to make things right with your child, diffuse any potential damage and reconnect and reset. Chapter 10 focuses on taming the storm and coping in the moment – also known as 'how to not throw your own tantrums and what to do if you do'.

Finally, Chapter 11 ties everything up and provides a refresher of previous chapters, before you embark on your own journey to calmer parenting, and rid yourself of those parenting tantrums you've become so accustomed to.

Chapter 1

Shadows from the Nursery –
Understanding Your Triggers
and Making Peace with
Your Own Childhood

*Deep in your wounds are seeds, waiting to grow
beautiful flowers.*

Niti Majethia, writer, editor and
spoken-word activist

How many times have you asked yourself, 'What's wrong with me? Why can't I be calm?' I've worked with so many parents over the last two decades who tell me that they would love to follow a gentler, more positive style of parenting, but that they don't think they're cut out for it because they aren't naturally calm. They feel that there is something wrong with them, that they're not good enough. They believe they are somehow failing their children by not controlling their own emotions adequately, no matter how hard they try. What these people don't realise, however, is that this describes almost every parent there ever was – and ever will be.

To be calm, we must understand everything that inhibits and triggers us. Sometimes it's easy to recognise these triggers.

Sometimes it's simple to work out what is inhibiting our emotion control – very often it's external factors in our daily lives or interactions with the people who are close to us (two things we will discuss in later chapters). Sometimes, however, these triggers and inhibitions have their roots deep inside us, in a place that we have long since left physically, but emotionally still has an immense hold on us: our own childhoods.

Some of us will be aware of traumatic events in our childhoods, others may not. For those in the latter category, it may not be one large event, but rather a collection of small moments, conversations, comments or experiences that, individually, may seem inconsequential, but added together can have a huge impact on our developing psyches. The shadows from our nurseries – our experiences during our formative years – are not necessarily about the things that happened to us, but the feelings they elicited in us as children and our perception of them. What is stressful or traumatic to one child may not be for another, and vice versa. Trauma is unique and personal.

Our inner voices and the words that ultimately leave our mouths when we respond to our children, particularly in times of heightened emotions, are often subconscious memories of the way we were spoken to as children. Some people were lucky enough to be treated with empathy and respect by their caregivers, and they tend to find it easier to respond to their children with an air of calm and cool. For others, however, who did not experience respect or understanding, the default response is often to repeat the same authoritarian words and actions they themselves heard as children. In childhood, many of us felt somehow responsible for our parents' and other caregivers' emotions. We learned, whether rightly or wrongly, that if we were quiet and not needy (often referred to as 'being good'), then our parents and caregivers were calm and happy. If we were somehow 'naughty' (for instance, if we were particularly needy, or had trouble regulating our emotions), then their moods were more likely to be angry. This subconscious belief can – and does – often lead to children repressing their own emotions or needs in the mistaken conviction that they are unlovable and unlikeable if they are struggling. This learned, erroneous behaviour from the past can become a huge trigger for us as adults, when our own children misbehave, because somewhere deep inside us is a lost child crying for attention, but one who has learned to repress their needs. When our own children act in a similar needy or dysregulated way, it triggers us not only because of their needs, but because of our own past needs, too.

It isn't just the interactions with our children that are impacted by our own past, though. The way we were raised can leave an indelible imprint on the conversations we have with ourselves, our self-beliefs and the exchanges and relationships we have with others. Perhaps you grew to question your self-worth? Perhaps you struggle with perfectionism and are highly self-critical? Or maybe you have an inability to trust others to complete a task as well as you and end up overwhelmed and exhausted with shouldering the burden alone, as a result? Perhaps you find it difficult to share your worries or concerns with others, or to ask for help when you're struggling? Or perhaps you are a 'people pleaser', always saying 'yes' when you'd really love to be able to say 'no'. If any of these descriptions rings true for you, it is highly likely that the roots of these beliefs and behaviours are in your very earliest years. You may have learned to keep everything inside because if you displayed your emotions you were banished to your room, or put in time out, as punishment. Or you struggle with perfectionism and self-worth because of a struggle to measure up to your siblings, or years spent in a quest for parental adoration, praise and attention. Or you were raised to believe that other people's needs mattered more than your own and that you should always try to keep others happy, no matter how unhappy it made you.

These imprints on our psyches start at the very beginning of our lives and can shape who we become as adults, whether we have children of our own or not. They can impact our future adult relationships and the ease with which we can sit with our own company and self-talk. The impact doesn't end there, though, as one simple word, phrase or behaviour from our own children can become a huge trigger to us, if it subconsciously reminds us of being a child or strikes us in the heart of our vulnerabilities. This, in turn, can result in a reaction from us that is hugely out of proportion to what our child has said or done – because it isn't about them; it's about us.

We will look at these self-beliefs in more detail a little later in this chapter, before ending with real, tangible actions you can take to heal some of your past wounds to ensure you don't pass them on to your children. In short, though, we need to change our inner dysfunctional, damaged voices to ones that are more understanding, more supportive and more mature. We need to examine what we believe the relationship of parent and child should look like, and what respect in this relationship truly means. And the good news is that it is possible, albeit not easy, to make these changes by firstly showing ourselves the kindness and empathy that we perhaps didn't fully receive as children – something that is summed up by Dr Bessel van der Kolk in his book *The Body Keeps the Score*:

Neuroscience research shows that the only way we can change the way we feel is by becoming aware of our inner experience and learning to befriend what is going inside ourselves.

Is this all about shifting blame onto your own parents?

Before we move on, I need to take a moment to reassure you that working to heal your inner child is not the same as blaming your parents or souring your relationship with them. You can still love your parents – deeply – while recognising that you experienced trauma in your childhood. It doesn't have to be one or the other. For some, that relationship may have already ended or become toxic, but the aim with investigating and healing from your past isn't to create negativity or relationship problems if your parents are still in your life. Far from it. Instead, it's about increasing the empathy you have for them.

We need to recognise that, for most of us, our parents were doing the best they could with the way they themselves were raised. Just as being kind to ourselves is imperative when working towards calmer parenting, seeing our parents' and caregivers' flaws and mistakes when raising us as issues they inherited from their own parents, rather than being caused by something we did, is so helpful. It's not about blaming our parents (or our grandparents), rather it's about understanding them and why they said and did what they did when you were young. Our parents and caregivers are as much products of their own upbringings as we are; the only difference is that we live in a culture and time now that is aware of childhood trauma, so we can be the generation to break the cycle. Our parents and caregivers weren't so lucky.

What lurks beneath

In the early twentieth century, the Austrian neurologist and founder of psychoanalysis, Sigmund Freud, introduced his model of the mind,[1] divided into three sections, as per the diagram below:

The conscious mind contains all the thoughts, feelings and decisions that we are fully aware of. For example, if you feel hungry and decide to make yourself some food, this is a conscious decision.

The preconscious mind contains memories that can be readily recalled, although they are not in our conscious minds every day. It is an area of the mind the individual is not immediately aware of, but it is not repressed and can be easily accessed.

The unconscious mind contains thoughts, feelings and memories that are not accessible to the conscious mind, often because the individual has repressed them due to hurt or fear. These thought processes are, according to Freud, the primary influence of conscious behaviour.

In the case of our childhoods influencing our interactions with our own children, when we try to follow parenting advice, we are accessing our conscious minds, or sometimes the preconscious. Nevertheless, we still struggle to respond in the way we would like, and anger, frustration and intolerance rear their ugly heads. This is a classic example of Freud's unconscious mind impacting on conscious behaviour – your unconscious being the area of your mind where all the negative and hurtful experiences of your childhood live (see diagram above). To become calmer, you must be mindful of the influence of these early events and actively work to uncover and understand the beliefs and experiences that drive you.

Although Freud's theories have been criticised for being too simplistic, they are helpful when we are trying to work on becoming calmer. As one of Freud's contemporaries, the Swiss psychiatrist and psychoanalyst Carl Jung, said, 'Until you make the unconscious conscious, it will direct your life and you will call it fate.' The good news, however, is that we can make a start on becoming more conscious today, the first hurdle being to acknowledge that we all carry with us hurtful words, events and actions from our childhoods and that these can often impact our everyday interactions with our children.

What parents say

When researching and writing this book I spoke to many parents. I asked what triggered their anger and made it hard for them to be calm parents. Here's what some of them had to say about their own upbringings and how these impacted their parenting:

> When my son is speaking to me disrespectfully it makes me see red. I know some of this is due to how I was raised and what would have happened to me if I had dared to speak to my parents like that.

> I struggle to parent calmly and empathetically when I'm still processing unresolved childhood trauma inflicted by my own caregivers.

> When I was naughty as a child I was sent up to my room and told to stay there until I was calm. I'm sure this has affected me into adulthood. I really struggle to ask for help

if I'm having a hard time and find it hard to open up about my feelings.

I really crave being seen or validated, and I am easily triggered by feeling that nobody cares about my needs. This ties in with resentment towards my partner when he can sit down and do his own thing quite often, whereas I am constantly interrupted by our children. It looks back to feeling ignored and abandoned when I was a child.

I was taught that 'grown-ups should always be respected' as a child and accepted it without question, but looking back now I realise that nobody respected me as a child, and I think this has caused some self-esteem issues as an adult.

My parents always used to tell me to stop crying when I was a child. I don't know if this is why I find it hard to let out my emotions now, but I suspect it hasn't helped. I think it also really triggers me when my own children cry, because I know I would have got into trouble for that as a child myself.

Adverse childhood experiences (ACEs)

In recent years, there has been a growing awareness of the impact of traumatic experiences in early childhood, known as 'adverse childhood experiences' (ACEs) on the future mental and physical health of the individual. Traumatic experiences in childhood, especially during the first few months when we are not aware of what has happened to us, but we are learning to build trust, alongside our rapidly developing brains and nervous systems, can cause our bodies to remain in an almost constant state of high alert. In a sense, our bodies and minds are waiting for the next threat to appear, and if we do not receive adequate soothing and regulation from parents and caregivers in infancy and childhood, then we struggle to learn how to regulate ourselves as adults. The absence of a calm, wise, supportive and regulated adult caring for us, with a calm and mature nervous system to match, means that we can find it incredibly difficult to learn these all-important regulation skills, not just because of a lack of modelling, but because we tend to live in a survival state. A state where we push our own needs and feelings to the back of our minds and focus instead on just getting through the day. In this state, we do not learn to identify our needs, let alone meet them, and we do not learn how to resolve or regulate stress levels. Sadly, this leaves children unable to escape both the traumatic situation and their stressful emotions or feelings. As a child grows, they learn to keep their feelings buried; they learn to survive at the expense of thriving. And if they continue to carry these big feelings and difficult buried emotions with them into adulthood, they can spill out at unexpected times. Often, our reaction is completely out of sync with our child's actions – something many would term an overreaction; however, we are not just responding to our child's actions and emotions, but those deep inside ourselves, too.

A good way to visualise this is with the illustration overleaf. It depicts an adult holding a bucket, which is full to the brim of the regular stresses and strains of everyday life, alongside a good dose of unresolved trauma and emotions from their own childhood. The adult may be just about managing, holding the bucket straight and working hard not to spill any of the contents. However, if their child bumps into them (and by a bump, I mean any behaviour that triggers the adult to lose control of their full bucket – a tantrum, answering back, ignoring requests and so on), the adult will inevitably spill some of what is in their bucket onto the child. The contents of that spill are largely unrelated to the child's actions and often not proportionate to the child's actions. But because the adult has been working so hard to keep everything in their bucket, it is almost impossible to stop some of the contents sloshing out.

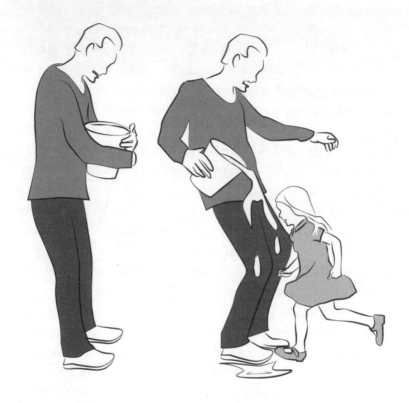

What qualifies as an ACE? And what is the impact?

According to the CDC-Kaiser Permanente Adverse Childhood Experiences Study,[2] there are ten specific ACEs, covering physical and verbal abuse:

1. Receiving verbal/emotional abuse from a parent/carer as a child

2. Being physically abused as a child

3. Being sexually abused as a child

4. Growing up with physical neglect (for example, a lack of food, clean clothing, etc.)

5. Growing up with emotional neglect (for example, a lack of love and nurturance)

6. Growing up in a home with a parent/carer with mental-health issues

7. Growing up in a home with a parent/carer who was a victim of domestic abuse

8. Growing up in a home with divorced or separated parents

9. Growing up in a home with a parent/carer with substance abuse (for example, alcoholism/drug addiction)

10. Growing up in a home with a parent/carer who was in prison

According to the study, 61 per cent of adults have gone through a minimum of one ACE, with at least one in six experiencing at least four individual ones. The research found that those who had suffered ACEs were more likely to have physical and mental-health problems in adulthood and to see a negative impact on their education and career prospects.

There has, however, been widespread dispute over the list, the main arguments being that it is too restrictive and that it is based on evidence from predominantly white, middle-class individuals, so is not inclusive. It also oversimplifies a complex and highly nuanced issue. As I've said, trauma is unique to the individual: some of us may find things traumatic that others may not and vice versa. Similarly, there may not have been one large traumatic event, but rather several smaller ones that collectively create a much larger issue. We may have grown up with a parent – or parents – who, on paper, were loving and caring, and we may feel that we had a positive relationship with them with no discernible ACEs; however, we can still feel, either at the time or retrospectively, that we were inadequately supported or didn't receive the necessary validation as a child.

Finally, many view the ACEs movement as a foregone conclusion that those who identify one or more ACEs will go on to develop problems in adulthood, which is not true. ACEs identify risks, not predetermined life paths. While being aware of them is incredibly important, not least in the quest to try to prevent them in the first place, it is also imperative that we don't automatically presume that a child will grow to become a certain person with certain issues because of what happened to them in childhood; this promotes a defeatist attitude that can, ultimately, be more harmful to children, and indeed to us, as grown adults. We can change. I myself score a two on the ACEs questionnaire, but I do not feel that my life is constrained by my traumatic childhood experiences. In fact, I think they are what drives me to do the work I do today with such passion.

While undoubtedly impacted by what happened to you in your childhood, your future is not outside of your control, and no questionnaire or, indeed, research, can tell you what the rest of your life will look like, what type of a person you are now or who you can be in the future.

The flight, fight, fawn and freeze responses

The events and experiences of your childhood don't just impact your emotions and their regulation and manifestations – they can have a significant effect on your physical wellbeing, too. Most of us are aware of the 'fight-or-flight' response: our bodies' physiological response to a real or perceived threat. When we feel in danger, our sympathetic nervous system stimulates our adrenal glands to secrete catecholamines – chemicals known as neurotransmitters – because they send signals to other cells, such as adrenaline and noradrenaline. The secretion of these neurotransmitters causes the body to get ready to fight (either physically or verbally – with lots of yelling) or take flight (run away), by increasing breathing, heart rate and blood pressure. You may also notice that your mouth feels dry, your body starts to tremble, your digestive system is altered (perhaps causing diarrhoea), your skin feels clammy and you may look pale or flushed. These physical signs and reactions are all part of the process of your body getting ready to preserve your life by running or fighting. Once the threat (or your perception of a threat) passes, it takes between half an hour and an hour for your body to return to its pre-stress levels. Most of us can recognise these responses easily, especially when it comes to fraught exchanges with our children. We can feel the red mist rising, and if we take a moment to be aware, we can feel our muscles tightening, our jaws clenching, our pulse rising and our breathing speed up and become shallower. These responses often precede a loss of emotional control, or what I term a parent tantrum. If we can notice them a little earlier, we can take steps to let our bodies know that the threat is only perceived and that we are safe – something we will talk about a little later in this chapter.

While awareness of the fight-or-flight response is pretty widespread, most adults are less aware of the freeze and fawn responses. The freeze response to stress causes us to feel stuck, both physically and emotionally. It is like the fight-or-flight response in that it is automatic, or out of our conscious control, and can manifest in a sense of being physiologically frozen to the spot, when you find it hard to move your limbs, or you subconsciously hold your breath. Alternatively, you may experience more psychological symptoms, including a struggle with speaking or finding the right words, or feeling fuzzy and unable to think clearly or remember anything well. From an evolutionary perspective, the freeze response is akin to playing dead in the face of a threat and tends to occur as a form of self-protection over time. It is more likely to occur if the person who is attacking (or perceived to be attacking) you is significantly larger and stronger than you – in a parent-and-child situation, for instance. You may remember a time in your childhood where you felt threatened, not just physically but verbally and emotionally, too, by an adult, and subconsciously your body decided it would be best for you to freeze as a response. Now, as an adult, you may look back at the situation and think, 'Why didn't I say something?' or 'Why didn't I tell them to stop?' However, this sort of retrospection completely misses the very real physical and emotional impact of the freeze response at the time. You didn't because you *couldn't*.

But how could this impact your relationship with your children? Well, you may find yourself entering this state if you feel somehow threated by their words or actions, or even those of others, if they are onlookers. Or perhaps you may find yourself in a similar situation to one you found yourself in as a child, which subconsciously triggers the freeze response. You may struggle to know how to react and once the moment passes, you may chastise yourself for having not known what to do, or for not being a better parent, without recognising the difficult physical and emotional state you found yourself in.

The final response, the fawn response, is perhaps the least known of all four stress or trauma responses. It occurs when an individual feels threatened by another and instinctually, automatically, seeks to please the aggressor (or perceived aggressor). This response is a form of self-defence, or a protective mechanism, to shield the individual from further physical or verbal attack by the aggressor. In the case of a child and parent or caregiver interaction, the fawn response is likely to occur when the adult is abusive in some way, or disciplines in an authoritarian manner (discipline with fear and punishment). To avoid further emotional or physical hurt, the child disguises their fear and big emotions and seeks to placate and please the adult. Although maladaptive (not healthy), this response to stressors (or the perception of them) can and often does continue into adulthood. It can affect our adult relationships with romantic partners, friends and colleagues, often resulting in burying our own emotions and needs in the quest to keep others happy. More commonly known as 'people pleasing', fawning behaviours can also be carried with us into our relationships with our children – in the subconscious avoidance of conflict, we instead choose to bow down to our children, letting them get away with hurtful words and behaviours. This can then lead to us feeling more out of control, struggling with burying our own needs and emotions to such a point that we reach burnout, or an explosion when the pressure mounts too much. We'll talk more about your relationships with others, especially other adults, the curse of 'people pleasing' and how to meet and honour your own needs later in the book.

WHAT'S YOUR PREDOMINANT STRESS-RESPONSE STYLE?

Being aware of your predominant stress-response style helps you to identify and notice your typical reactions and can help you to regulate them. The following three questions can give you a little insight into your predominant style if you don't immediately recognise yourself in the previous descriptions.

Question 1

When you feel threatened or stressed by something, what physical sensation(s) do you tend to notice most in your body?

A. Tension and tightness in your jaw and muscles
B. An increased heart and breathing rate
C. A heaviness or numbness in part or all of your body
D. Nausea and butterflies in your stomach

Question 2

When you feel threatened or stressed by something, which of the following is the phrase most like the thoughts in your head?

A. 'I need to fight my corner; I am in control here.'
B. 'I need to keep myself busy; if I'm distracted, I won't be so stressed.'
C. 'I can't deal with this right now; I want everybody to leave me alone.'
D. 'I would rather they were happy, even if it means not putting my point across.'

Question 3

How do you think your friends and family would describe you in times of stress?

A. 'Prone to shouting and yelling.'
B. 'Tends to be quite panicky and rushes around a lot; always on the go.'
C. 'Tends to retreat into themselves, shutting others out.'
D. 'Always worried about how others feel and actively avoids conflict.'

If you answered:
mostly As: yours is mostly a 'fight' stressor style
mostly Bs: yours is mostly a 'flight' stressor style
mostly Cs: yours is mostly a 'freeze' stressor style
mostly Ds: yours is mostly a 'fawn' stressor style.

The polyvagal theory

In the 1990s, American psychiatrist Dr Stephen Porges introduced his idea of the polyvagal theory.[3] Humans possess twelve pairs of cranial nerves that connect the brain with other parts of the body. One of these, the vagus nerve, serves to connect the brain with the heart, lungs and gastrointestinal system – the parts of the body most involved in the classic fight-or-flight response. The vagus nerve (or rather pair of nerves) is the longest cranial nerve in the body, originating in the brain stem and running past the ears, down the neck and then moving down the thorax (the area of our ribs) before finally terminating in the abdomen.

Porges believes that the vagus nerve not only gives rise to the fight-or-flight response but can also calm it by triggering a state of relaxation. He believes that if we stimulate the vagus nerve and focus on moving from a state of stress and tension to a state of relaxation, we can cause a physiological response by making the body believe that it is safe. This sounds entirely plausible to me; however, the polyvagal theory has plenty of detractors. The most pervasive criticism is the lack of evidence to back the claims; however, regardless of the lack of evidence base, I find it an incredibly helpful concept to embrace as a parent because it gives us very real and tangible actions to follow, to restore us to a state of calm.

So how do you make your body feel safe and stimulate your vagus nerve (often referred to as improving vagal tone)? The following are all simple and quick techniques you can employ in times of stress:

- Focus on slowing your breathing down, taking fewer breaths per minute and making your exhalation breath longer than your inhalation.
- Focus on breathing more deeply, with each breath starting deep in the belly (otherwise known as 'diaphragmatic' or 'belly' breathing) and expanding the whole of the ribcage as you breathe in.
- Gargling, humming, or singing loudly stimulate your vocal cords, which are located close to your vagus nerve.
- Using cold exposure, such as a thirty-second blast of cold water at the end of your shower.

Regardless of the critics, the polyvagal theory is something I always recommend stressed parents read up on; at the very least, they will spend a few moments a day being mindful of their breathing, while at best, they may create a huge difference in their stress responses, making their bodies feel safer which, in turn, will impact the way they interact with their children, making them feel calmer and safer, too. As Dr Porges says, 'If you want to improve the world, start by making people feel safer.'

How do you heal from childhood wounds?

The good news is that it is totally possible to learn to identify and heal from hurtful experiences in your childhood. The bad news is that there is no quick fix. Your goal is to first make any traumatic events or negative conditioning conscious. This awareness is the most important step because being mindful of who we are, what has happened to us and how our past impacts us in the present day allows us to put in place a personal plan for the future. Once you become more conscious of the effects of your childhood on your interactions with your children, the next step is to learn to react and respond in a more regulated way. This requires you to find a safe outlet for any pain and hurt, allowing the big, repressed emotions within you to finally dissipate. There is no one-size-fits-all way to do this – some prefer to utilise therapeutic techniques, professional counselling and therapy, while others choose to use movement or exercise, art or music or self-guided visualisations, affirmations or mindfulness techniques. The one element that underpins all these, however, is the importance of being kind to yourself – something we will look at much more in Chapter 9.

If you are unsure of where to start or the best route for you, the following five points can help. Together, they spell the word CHILD, in recognition of the child within you.

- Consciousness: acknowledge the trauma and its impact on you.
- Honour your emotions and allow yourself to feel them all in a safe way. Recognise the difference between being authentically you versus pushing away emotions and putting on a mask for others.
- Investigate your triggers, notice your stress responses and

tune in to your body's reactions. What can you learn about yourself in interactions with your child?

- Link up with others who can support and guide you on your journey; this may be a mental-health professional, a support group or social media contacts who help you to feel safe and inspired.
- Define small, realistic and achievable goals. Allow time and patience with yourself, aiming for repeated small steps, not giant leaps.

What parents say

I asked some parents what helped them to heal from childhood wounds. Here are some of their answers:

Not stuffing down emotions that are inconvenient or uncomfortable, only for them to erupt in moments when I'm triggered. I try to process them through journaling, talking to a friend or a counsellor.

Therapy to understand my past. Honesty. Being able to be vulnerable (in a safe space). Self-compassion. Nurturing my inner child and getting my needs met all help.

I like to imagine talking to my childhood self and telling her that she is enough, that it's not her fault, that she will grow to be a happy, confident and loved adult.

It really helps me to remember that my parents were doing the best that they could with the information they had available to them at the time. It sort of helps me to realise that they weren't consciously seeking to mess me up!

Just being patient with myself. Realising that we're all a little messed up and that's OK; we're all works in progress.

Some exercises to help you on your healing journey

To get you started, I have included ten exercises to help you think about your triggers and work towards diffusing any hurt that may stem from your past. You don't need to do all of them, just pick the one(s) that feel right for you. You may do one or two now and come back to this chapter in the coming weeks and months; there is no right or wrong way – just whatever works for you. If you do find an exercise particularly useful, it can also be a good idea to record and date your answers today and then revisit them, repeating the exercise in a month or two, to assess any change in the way you think and feel.

EXERCISE 1: Identify your key triggers

As I've mentioned throughout this chapter, awareness – or consciousness – of your past experiences and how they shape you today, especially as an adult, is the most important step you can ever take towards healing. In this exercise, we will look at what could possibly be behind your behaviours and limiting beliefs. As you read through each line of the table, you can mark the final column with a D (**D**efinitely applies to me), M (**M**aybe applies to me) or an N (**N**o, that's not me). There are a couple of blank lines at the end of the table for you to add any of your own behaviours and triggers you can identify.

Behaviour or belief	Possible underlying triggers	Does this apply to you?
Needing to be liked by others	Validation seeking, due to not receiving unconditional love as a child Being raised with too much superficial praise; self-worth based on what others think of you	
People pleasing (dismissing your own needs to meet those of others)	Being taught to be polite to others, no matter how you felt Expected to be 'good' and compliant as a child, changing your behaviour to please adults	
Attempts to avoid conflict	Always being taught to obey as a child, with an expectation children should be submissive Being punished as a child when you showed your authentic self or attempted to 'answer back' to explain your position or voice your disagreement	
A sense of rage or indignance when your child is rude to you	Being chastised or punished for voicing your opinions Being raised with a belief that adults are always right and more deserving of respect than children	

Behaviour or belief	Possible underlying triggers	Does this apply to you?
Constant comparison between yourself and others	Feelings and needs ignored in childhood, therefore validation sought in adulthood Raised with comparison between yourself and siblings (with the sibling being favoured)	
Perfectionism	Lack of recognition for trying, with praise and rewards only heaped on you when you achieve excellence Unrealistic demands made of you and your behaviour, leading to a fear of failure Not receiving appropriate emotional support in times of need, resulting in a sense of shame if you are unable to cope alone	
Tidiness obsession	An attempt to be in control of an environment or situation that you had little control over as a child Being raised by parents who struggled with perfectionism and comparison themselves (with the subconscious belief that tidiness is somehow a measure of worth)	

Behaviour or belief	Possible underlying triggers	Does this apply to you?
An inability to relax/taking on too much	Discipline approaches involving distraction methods, to avoid focusing on and dealing with your emotions Predominant 'flight' stress response, in reaction to stressful situations at home	
Difficulty trusting others	Growing up without a confidante to listen to your fears and worries Not being able to trust anybody to help you as a child, leaving you to grow to believe that the only person you can rely upon is yourself; often linked to perfectionism	
Avoiding putting yourself in vulnerable positions	Raised to not discuss or dwell on emotions as a child, with an emphasis on being strong – e.g. 'man up', 'be brave', 'big girls don't cry!' Being punished or excluded when showing your authentic self and true emotions as a child	

Behaviour or belief	Possible underlying triggers

EXERCISE 2: Body scan

Being aware of the sensations within our bodies – particularly as we feel our stress levels start to rise and the first bubbles of anger or frustration – can help us to spot early warning symptoms in the future, enabling us to proactively take steps to calm ourselves down. Try to check in with yourself when you're feeling calm and notice:

- How does your jaw feel?
- How are your shoulders sitting?
- How fast is your heart beating?
- How does the skin on your palms feel?
- What sensations do you notice in your abdomen?
- How do your legs feel?
- Where is your breath originating from?
- Can you feel yourself holding tension anywhere in your body?
- Are you hydrated enough?

The next time you start to feel difficult emotions or find yourself in a tricky situation with your child, allow yourself a minute to check in with your body again, asking the same questions. What differences do you notice? Can you imagine any part of your body that is holding on to tension loosening and relaxing? If you regularly practise focusing on relaxation, it will ultimately allow you to become calmer.

EXERCISE 3: Write a letter to the past you

Sit down with a pen and paper or a laptop or tablet, if you prefer, and write a letter to your child self. Pick a year that you feel would benefit the most, perhaps your three-year-old, five-year-old, ten-year-old or even eighteen-year-old self. (Ask yourself which age needs your help the most and trust the first answer that instinctively comes to mind.) Start your letter with the words 'Dear me at age xx' (fill in as applicable). Then consider what would you want your child self to know? Or what would you like to hear them say to you in a letter in reply? Imagining what your child self would say in reply can help you to tune in to feelings that you may have buried and repressed.

Once you've completed this letter, ask yourself if you feel the need to write to yourself at a different age and repeat the process, until you feel that the exercise is complete.

EXERCISE 4: Turn criticisms into compliments

What criticisms did you receive as a child from your parents or other important caregivers in your life? Write each of these down. Once you have finished, take a bold pen and use it to cross each of the criticisms out and write a new, positive word about yourself in its place.

EXERCISE 5: Re-parent yourself

Close your eyes and imagine revisiting yourself in your past, choosing a moment in time when you feel you would have really benefited from some support or sage advice. What comes to mind? Just let the memories pop up. Now imagine yourself as you are now – an adult – standing next to your child self. Think about what you would say to yourself in this moment as an older, wiser adult. What advice would have helped you? What could you say or do to reassure past you? Would giving your child self a big hug help? Or perhaps you could create a safe space – a space to cry and let your feelings out. Move through different times and periods from your childhood that pop into your mind and when you feel you could really have benefited from mature, regulated and supportive input from an adult. Those fears and worries are likely still inside you now, but you can start to heal them by applying your own advice to the inner child you.

EXERCISE 6: Identify your erroneous parenting beliefs

What beliefs did you grow up with about parenting? What expectations have you carried with you into your own role as a parent? Where do you think these beliefs stem from? And, most importantly, are they accurate and helpful?

For instance, do you believe that a good parent doesn't yell? Or maybe, a good parent's children are not disrespectful?

Perhaps you believe that a good parent never struggles? Or that a good parent should have a tidy and organised home?

By taking a moment to analyse the origins and accuracy of these beliefs in this way you can take enormous pressure off yourself as a parent.

EXERCISE 7: Tell your body it is safe

Picking up on the polyvagal theory (see page 27) and continuing with the work of exercise 2, this time you are going to focus on ways that you can convince your body and nervous system that you are safe, especially the next time you start to feel triggered. This can include:

- taking deep, slow breaths in, focusing on expanding your abdomen with each inhalation
- counting through your in and out breaths, making sure your out breath is longer than your in breath
- gently humming or making an 'ohm' sound in your throat
- purposefully and slowly moving in a series of stretches or similar
- being aware of the sensations of the ground beneath your feet and feeling a connection to the earth, focusing on the gentle pull of gravity
- repeating in your mind 'I am safe, I am secure'.

EXERCISE 8: Who am I really?

Take a pen and paper or open notes on your PC or phone and ask yourself the question: 'Who am I away from the beliefs and expectations of everybody else?' What makes you happy? What makes you fulfilled? What makes you passionate? Learning to be authentic and understanding your true self, away from the pressures and expectations of others is an important step towards becoming fulfilled and happy with yourself.

EXERCISE 9: Find your support network

This exercise is important because it's all about planning a support network. This doesn't have to be friends and family. In fact, it doesn't even have to include people you've met in real life. But you do need to plan a network you can turn to if you are struggling. It could be virtual friends or support groups. Or it could be a professional therapist or counsellor. Using the Resources section at the back of this book as a starting point, write a bullet point list of organisations and individuals you could reach out to, or investigate, to help provide you with a support network.

EXERCISE 10: Future you, present you

Close your eyes and imagine yourself ten years into the future. Ten years along this journey. Ten years more wisdom. Ten years more practice at becoming calmer, freeing yourself of the expectations and beliefs of others. Ten years of living authentically. Look at the way you hold yourself, your facial expressions and the way you move. Listen to the tone of your voice and the words that you say. What does future you have to say to current you? Do they have any advice for you? Can you imagine stepping into their body and feeling the new sense of calm, purpose and understanding that they have. This is what you are working towards. This is who you can become. It's not some unrealistic comparison or expectation. This is you! Listen to future you as they tell you that you can do it. You can become the person and parent you want to be.

What about conversations with your own parents?

So far, we have focused on working on yourself, on your own inner dialogues. Should you have conversations with your parents if they are still alive? Sometimes conversations with your parents or caregivers will help you to heal, but sometimes they will make everything, and everyone, feel worse. There is no right answer here. Sometimes I consider myself lucky that both of my parents died when I was in my early twenties, before I became a parent myself or had much time for introspection, as now I am only left with the option of empathising with them and trying to understand their words and actions. Would I have had a conversation with them about difficult parts of my childhood if they were still alive? I honestly don't know. But I do believe that the decision to do so has to be made while considering your own unique situation and whether, ultimately, the conversation will aid or hinder your healing. The one thing that you must remember is that none of this work is about blame.

In brief

As we come to the end of this chapter, I want to recap on a few of the most salient points we have discussed:

1. Being aware of what happened to you in your own childhood – what has shaped you into the person you are today – should always be your starting point in your journey to calmer parenting.

2. This awareness should hopefully lead to an understanding of your biggest triggers. What behaviour from your child – or from others – sparks a disproportionate reaction from you? What lies beneath this response? Why is this a trigger?

3. You must be kind to yourself. This is vulnerable work and to do it you need to feel safe, which means taking things slowly. It can be hard sometimes to acknowledge what happened to you as a child and to sit with those memories and feelings.

4. Your goal is to fully accept yourself – the good and (what you think is) the bad – and slowly work towards releasing any thoughts and beliefs that no longer serve you.

What should you expect in terms of healing? Well, you certainly shouldn't expect to become a totally new person. That's not feasible or realistic and it also should not be your aim. Your goal should be to become the best version of yourself by being more accepting of who you are – and, importantly, of where you came from.

Working through difficult experiences of your childhood puts you in a vulnerable position and can be uncomfortable. You may have developed a defence mechanism to avoid these sorts of feelings, or you may find that during the process you rely on previously used coping mechanisms and behaviour patterns that are unhealthy – for instance, comfort eating or becoming more insular. Try to recognise these behaviours as they occur and acknowledge that they are unproductive and no longer serve you or the person you wish to become. Reassure yourself that you are doing huge and important work and it's OK to feel scared at times. Try to sit with those feelings and allow them to be, rather than chasing them away.

Finally, and most importantly, recognise that you are a work in progress. Big change doesn't happen overnight. Setting goals for yourself that are unrealistic will lead to failure and frustration when you don't meet them. Aiming for tiny steps repeatedly is so much more helpful than expecting yourself to be the ultimate zen parent overnight. Which is a good point at which to leave this chapter now and move on to Chapter 2, which is all about the lure of perfection and why, ultimately, it doesn't serve us.

The Quest for Parenting Perfection – Embrace Your Own Failures and Rid Yourself of Guilt

Embrace your vulnerability and celebrate your flaws; it will let you appreciate the world around you and make you more compassionate.
Masaba Gupta, fashion designer

'What would you say your biggest flaw is?' If you've ever been asked this question in a job interview – and who hasn't? – I wager that your answer was probably along the lines of, 'Actually, I'm a bit of a perfectionist.' It seems a good, if clichéd, answer, doesn't it? Because effectively you're saying, 'I have an incredibly high level of attention to detail, I will be totally focused on this job and I will smash any challenges you set me.' What employer wouldn't want that? Perfectionism is surely the only flaw that is considered a positive? But it isn't. It's damaging and dangerous, particularly when it comes to parenting.

Time and time again I come across parents who feel they are failing their children because they have flaws. They believe that if they are not always ready and able to meet their child's needs, then they are not good enough. Each failure, whether small or large, and however frequent or infrequent, is viewed as an indication that they can never meet their own high expectations. Many parents live in a perpetual and tortuous cycle of shame, guilt and regret – all because they uphold the unattainable goal of parenting perfection. If there is one trait that holds us back from becoming calmer parents, it is surely perfectionism.

The sad reality is that those who focus on perfectionism are undoubtedly good parents because they are so desperate to better themselves for the sake of their children. But that same perfectionism can also be their undoing. Perfection is nothing but an illusion, yet when it comes to parenting, perfect seems to be the goal to aim for. And if what we are aiming for is an illusion, we are all doomed to fail, yet the quest for perfection is rooted in the desperate desire to avoid failure. Thus, we enter a vicious circle of expectations and aims set too high, leading to unavoidable 'failure', then guilt, depression and dented self-esteem and confidence. All of which causes us to reassess our parenting skills and aim for the fallacy of perfect, each time driving our psyche down a little more, as that nagging voice in our heads whispers, 'You're just not good enough.' It is a toxic, debilitating cycle that we must break if we hope to be calmer.

What parents say

I spoke to some parents about how perfectionism negatively impacts their ability to be calm. Here's what they told me:

I struggle with the constant weight of expectation from every direction – my husband, my family, my friends, society, strangers, work, my childcare provider.

I struggle with the constant pressure I place on myself to get family life to run smoothly. Then the guilt of not feeling present with my children hits. Which then makes me feel pulled in too many directions, ultimately ending with a very busy, frazzled headspace.

I find my own inner dialogue stressful at times, especially when there isn't anything physical to show for my hard work. I berate myself and have to remind myself that I've been looking after three small children and they are all happy, but it's tough.

I get really frustrated when I can't be the type of parent I want to be. I'm really harsh on myself when I fail, or I don't measure up to my own expectations.

The nirvana fallacy

In the late 1960s, the economist Harold Demsetz introduced the term 'the nirvana fallacy' to describe the belief of there being an ideal, perfect norm and an imperfect, flawed one. Or, in other words, there is always a perfect solution to something and because of this presumed perfection, the alternative is, therefore, imperfect. This type of thinking views the world in black and white, without consideration of the infinite shades of grey in between. If we regard the world through the lens of nirvana, or perfection, we not only judge ourselves more harshly, but we become less likely to attempt to improve our parenting because we believe it's not worth trying – we can't possibly measure up to the ideal, perfect parent.

The constant striving for perfection and the inevitable subsequent failure, whether it's parenting or something else entirely, dents our self-esteem and confidence, and the resulting self-directed negativity increases stress levels, reduces our overall sense of wellbeing, raises all sorts of difficult feelings from our past and puts us into survival, or fight-or-flight, freeze or fawn mode. Simply put, perfectionism is the enemy of calm parenting.

Why is perfectionism so damaging for parents?

The downsides of perfectionism are many, especially when it comes to parenting. There is a huge body of research looking into the effects of perfectionism, and some of the findings include being:[1]

- Less likely to delegate tasks and jobs to others, for fear that they cannot measure up to your high expectations, leaving you juggling too many tasks yourself
- Less likely to accept mistakes that you make, meaning constant self-judgement of your own skills, abilities and actions, combined with little positive acceptance and self-congratulation for something done well
- Less likely to accept mistakes made by others, including partners, children and other family members, leading you to live in a hyper-critical state, which can cause friction in relationships
- More likely to compare yourself to others, under the illusion that they can achieve perfection, so there must be something wrong with you for not being able to do the same
- More likely to burn out – because the unattainable expectations you set yourself, the huge workload (both mental and physical) taken on in order to try to achieve them and the tendency to overcontrol mean that you are far less likely to share the load you are carrying
- More likely to feel dissatisfied with your life and your achievements, if you don't consider them good enough

- More likely to have low self-worth and confidence and, as a result, more likely to suffer with depression and anxiety, due to the psychological burden of perfectionism
- In a constant state of hypervigilance and stress, always alert to the next potential failure; perfectionism can elicit a stressor response (fight-or-flight/freeze/fawn) and all that they entail
- More likely to practise helicopter parenting (constantly hovering over children and attempting to micromanage their every move)
- Less likely to enjoy parenting, with lower levels of satisfaction and increased stress, caused by not meeting the goals you've set for yourself
- More likely to struggle with meeting deadlines, tending towards procrastination and not completing things (if you are worrying about doing them perfectly, you are far less productive and sometimes may not even attempt a task, for fear of failure).

Perfectionism doesn't just affect us adults, though. If we are perfectionists, we are more likely to raise children who are perfectionists, too[2] – and thus more likely to identify with the points in this list as they grow up. Perfectionism is a familial trait that is passed on through the generations; you deserve to break the cycle for yourself, but if that isn't enough for you, break it for your children.

What underpins perfectionism?

As we learned in the previous chapter, a large majority of our behaviour as parents is rooted in our own childhoods and the way we ourselves were raised, as well as the relationships and interactions we had with our parents and caregivers. The origins of perfectionism are no exception to the rule here, and it is highly likely that your perfectionist behaviour is rooted in your past. Perhaps some of the following may ring true for you:

- You were a high achiever in childhood, either academically, in sports, or the arts.
- You were raised by a parent who lived vicariously through you, seeing your success as a measure of their own parenting or worth.
- You received lots of praise as a child when you achieved or succeeded at something, but your failures were punished or ignored.
- You received lots of material rewards in your childhood (such as certificates, badges, stickers, prizes and so on) when you did 'well', which created a subconscious association with feeling good only when achieving and succeeding at something.
- You were raised in a family who glossed over emotional problems and difficult feelings to seem perfect to others.
- You were raised to pursue unobtainable things, with goals and expectations that were advanced or unachievable for your age and abilities.
- You grew up feeling that how you behaved as a child somehow controlled how your parents felt and acted towards you – for instance, believing that if you were the perfect child, they would be happier or love you more, or their relationship with each other would be improved.
- As a child you were shamed or punished for your mistakes or excluded from the rest of the family, so you grew to associate love with perfection and the belief that being flawed made you unlovable.
- You were raised by a parent who believed that it was weak to need emotional support and, as such, you felt a sense of shame if you were unable to cope alone, leaving you with a strong desire to succeed without help.

- You didn't receive enough attention from your parents (for whatever reason) and grew to believe that if you were perfect, they would want to spend more time with you, especially because they could show you off to others.
- If you have siblings, you may have felt that you received more attention, and love, if you were a high achiever, especially if your sibling was too and you felt that you had to outdo, or at least match, them in achievement.
- You may have been raised by helicopter parents, who were constantly on high alert and warning you how bad it was to make a mistake.

But it isn't just our upbringing that leaves us vulnerable to perfectionism. We live in a consumerist society that preys on our imperfections and insecurities (perceived or real) to sell things. If we all accepted our unique flaws and had confidence in our abilities, looks and lives in general, we would be much harder to sell to. In fact, we would be a marketer's nightmare. It is much easier to sell a product or an idea to an audience who feel insecure and are constantly looking for that holy grail to reach the pinnacle of perfection. That's why most advertising is designed to undermine our self-esteem and feelings of contentment, and we voluntarily surround ourselves with these toxic messages constantly.

What else feeds into our desire to be perfect parents? We need to look at the value – or rather the lack of it – attached to child-raising today. Society and in particular governments today do not value childcare. Those who work in the childcare industry are hugely underpaid and their choice of career is often viewed as one for those who are unable to achieve higher paid, more intellectually demanding work. If you choose to be a stay-at-home parent, the media considers you to be lazy and a leech on society if you accept any state financial help. I can't tell you how many stay-at-home parents I have met who have introduced themselves as 'just a mum' or 'just a dad' when asked what their job is. It's almost as if they feel they must apologise for not contributing to national productivity and the public purse. Raising a tiny human, although possibly the hardest and most complex job in the world, is considered an easy, work-shy choice. This lack of societal value attached to child-rearing leaves us with the subconscious belief that we must somehow do it perfectly to prove the naysayers wrong – and prove to ourselves that we are 'worth it'.

The three main styles of perfectionism

In the late 1980s and 1990s, Canadian psychologists Paul Hewitt and Gordon Flett attempted to measure perfectionism with something they termed the Multidimensional Perfectionism Scale.[3] Using a questionnaire comprised of thirty-five questions, they ascertained the level of perfectionism an individual experienced. Their work led Hewitt and Flett to identify three prominent types of perfectionism:

1. **Self-orientated perfectionism** This is all about our self-talk. It encompasses an internal, often irrational desire to be perfect by living up to our own expectations of ourselves. This style could describe you if you identify with any of the following:

   - 'I set really high standards for myself and like to be the best at something.'
   - 'I always feel the need to give something my all, and then some.'
   - 'I can spend a lot of time analysing my behaviour and achievements and berating myself for not doing better.'

- 'Sometimes I procrastinate, or avoid doing something, because I'm scared of failing.'

2. **Other-orientated perfectionism** This is all about the standard we set and hold for others, and how we feel when they don't live up to our expectations. This style could describe you if you identify with any of the following:

   - 'I can be quite intolerant of my friends, family or colleagues if they make mistakes.'
   - 'I am often disappointed in others if they don't try hard enough or they put in less effort than me.'
   - 'I get frustrated with people who don't put effort or work into improving themselves or their situation.'
   - 'I feel let down by people when they don't complete something in a way that matches up to my high standards.'

3. **Socially prescribed perfectionism** This is all about living up to the expectations of others. It links our self-esteem and self-worth with what others think of us and the mistaken belief that everybody else expects us to be perfect. This style could describe you if you identify with any of the following:

   - 'I feel really bad if I let others down and don't do exactly what they ask.'
   - 'I feel a lot of pressure from others to do things really well all the time.'
   - 'I feel like if I was more successful, others would like and appreciate me more.'
   - 'I feel that the better I do, the better everybody expects me to be.'

Maybe you identify with one specific perfectionism style? Or perhaps you can see yourself in all three? (I have included information on how you can test your own perfectionism levels in the Resources section – see page 233). Self-orientated perfectionism is the most common type (and the one that I personally score the highest in, and struggle with), closely followed by socially prescribed perfectionism. Basically, we are far harder on ourselves than we are on others. When it comes to parenting, socially prescribed perfectionism is intricately linked with our sense of self-esteem and self-worth. Research has also found that the higher the level of a parent's socially prescribed perfectionism, the higher the chance that they will experience burnout and exhaustion.[4]

Is the key to calmer parenting therefore to somehow care less about the perceptions and expectations of others? I think so! One approach that may help here is to consider what has led to any parental 'failings' we may have had. While we are all quick to blame ourselves, saying, 'I'm not calm enough', 'I am bad at controlling my emotions', 'I find it hard to connect with my children' and so on, the truth is that the lack of support structures is to blame most of the time, specifically:

- the lack of a decent period of paid parental leave, so we can concentrate on our children, free of financial worries
- the lack of support for parents from family members
- the lack of support organisations for parents
- inadequate mental-health diagnosis, treatment and support services
- the lack of reliable, evidence-based, medical or professional childcare advice for parent.

The situation is compounded by:

- the constant conflicting parenting advice we receive

- advertising from companies designed to exploit our weaknesses and make us doubt ourselves.

None of the above is our fault, so why do we question ourselves and our abilities when we struggle? We are absolutely going to fall short of the expectations, or perceived expectations, of others, because it is impossible to meet them. There is an unwritten belief in our society that if we don't sail through parenting with ease, it must be because we are doing something wrong. Yet we don't question these messages. Instead, we automatically focus on our own flaws and proclaim that everything is our fault. I think the way forward is to recognise these expectations for the sham that they are and to understand that *everybody* feels as if they're messing up. The truth is, everyone is so worried about what others think of them that they have little time or energy to devote to judging others! If we could understand this, we would have a good chance of reducing our perfectionist tendencies. So how do we do this? On paper it sounds so simple: we turn the nirvana fallacy into a 'good enough' reality.

The good-enough parent

In the 1950s, the paediatrician and psychoanalyst Donald Winnicott introduced his idea of the 'good enough mother' to the British public, largely through a series of BBC radio broadcasts. Winnicott's work came at a time of huge transition after the end of the Second World War and his underlying message was a welcome one of support for parents, encouraging them to trust their instincts and reduce the burden of perfectionism. Winnicott believed that babies learn to develop independence primarily because of a series of small failures on the part of the mother to meet her baby's needs which, in turn, help the baby to know that they are safe without her. In Winnicott's own words: 'I would rather be the child of a mother who has all the inner conflicts of the human being than be mothered by someone for whom all is easy and smooth, who knows all the answers and is a stranger to doubt.'

Of course, despite the name, this idea isn't restricted to mothers; however, in the 1950s – when Winnicott named his concept – child-raising was almost solely the domain of mothers, hence the emphasis on mothering, rather than parenting. Society in the 1950s held the view that a woman's worth was (and arguably still is) linked to her ability to be a good housewife, a good wife and a good mother, with the subconscious messages from society to women conveying that they should somehow prioritise the roles of caregiver and caretaker over others. It makes sense, therefore, that Winnicott focused his attention on mothers, although his theories absolutely apply to fathers, too.

Despite seventy years having passed since Winnicott's broadcasts, modern research still supports his theories. In 2019, a study of parents and babies (aged between four and twelve months) looked at the parents' ability to provide comfort when their babies were crying.[5] It found that parents and caregivers only need to 'get it right' (i.e. respond appropriately with comfort and nurturance) 50 per cent of the time to have a positive impact on their babies. The study's lead researcher, Associate Professor of Counselling Psychology Susan S. Woodhouse, commented:

> It may be helpful for them to know that holding a crying infant until fully soothed, even 50 per cent of the time, promotes security … you don't have to do it 100 per cent – you have to get it right about half of the time, and babies are very forgiving and it's never too late. Keep trying. You don't have to be perfect; you just have to be good enough.

The concept of good-enough parenting is by no means just restricted to babies. It doesn't matter if your child is eight weeks, eight months, eight or even eighteen years old. As parents, it is imperative that we learn to fail with grace. We must understand that our failures are not just OK, but debatably more valuable than our parenting successes – because it is failure that is the precursor to learning and achievement, for both parent and child.

But why are our failures as parents so valuable to our children?

- Children need to learn how to mess up and how to apologise afterwards. The best way for them to learn this is to experience the same interaction with us.
- Children need to become disillusioned with their parents to facilitate independence and new relationships with others as they grow.
- Parents who make mistakes are more relatable and therefore better, far more realistic role models for children.
- Parents who aim for 'good enough', rather than perfection, are less likely to raise perfectionist children.

Sadly, the idea of 'good enough' is often associated with subpar parenting in our culture today. For some, it is used as an excuse for repeatedly prioritising their own needs over those of their children, rather than a more balanced approach where both needs are equally considered. However, 'good enough' is not the same as 'poor parenting'. It is not subpar; indeed, it carries benefits that 'perfect' parenting – if it were a real thing – does not. We must let go of the fallacy of the perfect or 'nirvana' parent. Instead, we must be prepared to welcome failure, to make peace with it and to view it as a learning and grounding opportunity – because failure is unavoidable in parenting. We must raise our children to be 'good enough', so that they don't carry with them our perfectionism.

How to move from perfectionism to good enough

The journey towards becoming a reformed perfectionist is a long one. However, the following seven exercises can help you to get started. As with the previous chapter, they aren't mandatory. If one or two don't work for you, then just move on to the next.

EXERCISE 1: Take an inventory of your thoughts

For this exercise, you will need to keep a list of your apparent 'failures' over the course of a few days or a week: if you feel that you have messed up in your parenting, write down what happened and your thoughts both during and after the event. After some time has passed, and the intensity of the feelings has faded a little, revisit your list and see if you can pinpoint any recurring themes, emotions or triggers. Recognising and, ultimately, understanding and accepting your mistakes is a huge leap forward in change. Being aware means you have done half of the work already!

EXERCISE 2: Revisit your past

Find somewhere comfortable and quiet to sit at a time when you feel otherwise relaxed, safe and secure. Close your eyes and revisit your childhood memories. Can you find one that is related to your perfectionism today? Perhaps you were at a school prizegiving ceremony; or you were sent to your room after a tantrum when you couldn't do something; or you overheard your parent boast about your achievements to somebody. Be aware of how you felt at the time and any thoughts that crossed your mind. What could you say to the child you were to help you to process this event differently?

EXERCISE 3: Reframe failure

Think back to a time when you received an award or a certificate and the pride you felt then. Now imagine that same pride, but this time you are receiving a 'failure award'. You are attending a failure-celebration ceremony and everybody is congratulating you for trying (albeit not succeeding), for your perseverance and for your continued learning. Perhaps you could make yourself a 'failure certificate' – print it out and stick it on your fridge.

EXERCISE 4: Positive affirmations

Choose a quiet time of the day when you have a couple of minutes' headspace to yourself – perhaps while you're showering in the morning, brushing your teeth at night, making packed lunches, commuting to work or running the vacuum cleaner around your home. Repeat the following statements to yourself, either in your mind or out loud – whatever works best for you. You could also print them out and stick them somewhere you will see them daily – on the back of your bathroom door, for instance.

- It is safe for me to fail.
- Perfect does not exist; good enough is more than enough.
- My child needs me to mess up to learn.
- I am enough as I am.
- Everyone makes mistakes.
- I accept my failures with grace.
- Authenticity is better than perfection.
- I am worthy of love, no matter how many mistakes I make.

Perhaps you can think of one or two more to add?

EXERCISE 5: Imagining the internal dialogue of others

Perfectionism fools us into believing that others don't struggle to achieve greatness, largely because it is far more common to share successes than failures. We only hear, see and feel our own struggles and so form the belief that we must be far less competent and calm than others. You are not weak or a bad parent if you have flaws, though. Imperfection is normal and nobody is flawless.

Realising that everybody struggles can help us to reduce the expectations we place upon ourselves. One of the best ways to do this is to imagine others, especially those we aspire to, experiencing the same self-doubt and negative internal chatter that we do. Pick somebody who you feel really has parenting nailed and imagine some of the doubts and anxiety they feel daily. If you have a close relationship with this person, you can also ask them to share their thoughts and feelings with you.

EXERCISE 6: Set yourself small, realistic, achievable goals

We know that perfectionism can often lead to procrastination and avoidance of doing something for fear of failure. Setting realistic goals is such an important step in your journey to calmer parenting. You must recognise and accept your limits and be realistic with expectations of yourself. Rather than jumping in and thinking, 'I'm going to be a calm parent by the end of the summer' or, 'I'm going to be totally different by the time I finish this book', focus on just one area at a time. For instance, 'For the next month, I'm going to work hard on accepting myself more and reducing my perfectionism a little.' You should also be realistic about time scales and what you can achieve; consistent small steps are far better than unpredictable big leaps. Try spending an hour or so thinking about your goals and writing them down. You can make them aspirational but dial back a little on the optimism to keep them realistic!

EXERCISE 7: Find the grey

Thinking back to the nirvana fallacy – the idea of black-and-white thinking, with perfect parenting at one end and bad parenting at the other, this exercise is all about seeing the shades of grey in between: the OK and the 'good enough'. If you find yourself reflecting on your parenting at the end of a day, don't just swing to either the perfect or the bad; instead, focus on the grey middle zone and reassure yourself that OK, or 'good enough' *is really* enough. It is likely to take many attempts until you feel comfortable in the grey zone, but the more you acknowledge its existence and validity, the easier it will be.

In brief

As we come to the end of this chapter, I want to recap on a few of the most important points around parenting perfectionism:

- Perfectionism is the enemy of calm parenting. It can force us into a state of stress and hypervigilance, causing us to spend more time in our stressor response. If your predominant response is 'fight mode', you are more likely to become angry and lose your temper at your children.
- Perfectionism makes you more liable to experience parenting burnout.
- Perfect parenting is a lie. The nirvana fallacy introduces us to the idea of the in between, the acceptable compromise of the grey zones. We can never achieve parenting perfection, but that doesn't mean we are bad parents.
- Perfectionism likely has its roots in your own childhood;

being aware of this and its impact on your current behaviour is the first step towards freeing yourself from the chains of perfectionism.

- Perfectionism is inherited: perfectionist parents are more likely to raise perfectionist children. Working on your perfectionism is not only good for you, but for your children, too.
- Good enough is better than perfect – it's not the poor relation. Being a good-enough parent teaches your child how to cope with failure and how to rectify mistakes and it encourages their independence. It also makes you more relatable as a role model.
- Reducing your perfectionism is a slow process. Perfectionists are prone to procrastination and putting off tasks if they think they are too hard. They are also more likely to give up if they fail at something. You must set yourself realistic goals, with baby positive steps, to avoid this.

I hope that this chapter has helped to provide some insight into any perfectionist tendencies you may have. I mentioned previously that I score very high on self-orientated perfectionism – quite literally, I am my own worst enemy. I also score higher than average on socially prescribed perfectionism, and at the heart of that, I think, is my tendency to compare myself to others – a trait that I know is incredibly common among the parents that I have worked with. For this reason, Chapter 3 is devoted entirely to the curse of comparison, and how it can thwart our efforts to be calmer parents.

Chapter 3

The Curse of Comparison – and Why it Hinders and Deceives Us

Stop thinking you're doing it all wrong. Your path doesn't look like anybody else's because it can't, it shouldn't, and it won't.

Eleanor Brownn, inspirational writer

Research has found that, on average, 12 per cent of our daily thoughts involve comparing ourselves to others.[1] From the moment we are born, we encounter comparison; we are weighed and measured and plotted on a centile chart. As we learn to crawl, sit up, walk and speak, our skills are constantly compared to our contemporaries'. We start school and our lives, our worth, are measured by percentages, test scores and homework grades. When we receive our exam results at age sixteen, we know exactly how we compare to the national average, which subjects we achieved higher in and which we fell short in. When we start work, we compare salaries, benefits, promotions and bonuses. When we have our own children, the comparisons come full circle, in a constant stream of questions – not just from others, but from our own minds, too: how much did he weigh at birth? How many hours does she sleep at night? When did he learn to walk? How many words can she say? Is my child where they should be? Have I done a good-enough job? Comparison is never-ending and we simply cannot escape it; it's ingrained in the very fabric of our lives. We live in a world that makes us constantly question: am I enough?

It's not necessarily what we see or hear when we compare ourselves – or our children – to others that's problematic, but our interpretation of it and how we twist it to mean something about ourselves. We weave stories about others, allowing our well-crafted myths to make ourselves feel we are not enough.

The biggest problem with all this is that when we compare, we are not treating like with like. We compare our reality to a fantasy version we have constructed of somebody else. It's the nirvana fallacy all over again (see page 45). We know ourselves inside and out. We know our own flaws and our failures, our worries and insecurities, and we presume that we know those of others. But we don't.

It's a little like a beautiful and intricate tapestry on display in a museum. It looks perfect to the viewer, sewn by highly skilled hands. But what you don't see when it hangs there in all its gorgeous glory is the mess of tangled knots on the back, pressed tightly to the wall, hidden from view. We are the back of the tapestry; others are the perfect front. The two are not comparable, yet we attempt to compare daily. We view ourselves subjectively and others objectively. But in reality, everybody else is as messed up as we are – they just don't advertise it.

Have you ever felt pleased with your work or proud of your parenting skills? Maybe you nailed a work presentation or came up with a great new activity idea that kept your child entertained for ages. You allowed yourself to feel happy. To feel the glow of achievement. But your triumph and glory were shattered all too soon because you found out somebody did it better than you. A colleague produced a superior presentation in less time, that was better received by the audience, or you opened your Instagram account and saw a sensory activity far more complex and engaging than your own. Suddenly you felt inferior. They were better than you; you were not good enough. And the pride and sense of achievement you had felt were quickly erased. Comparison can change your mood and your feelings about yourself in an instant.

How comparison can help us

Comparison isn't always bad, though. Here are some of the potential benefits:

- It helps us to keep a check on our children's milestones in relation to others of a similar age, and to seek help if we feel that they are outside the expected norm.
- In the context of other parents, it can sometimes inspire us to take on board some of their best bits to improve what we do.
- Comparing our current self to a past version of our self allows us to see how far we have come on a journey and can help us to feel proud of our efforts.
- It can help us to recognise and feel gratitude when we genuinely feel fortunate compared to others.
- If we are struggling with a specific parenting issue, comparison can sometimes help us to find solutions by observing what others have done differently when faced with a similar problem.
- We can use comparison to help us understand how others feel and increase our sense of empathy towards them.
- As we begin to understand others and what makes them tick, including our own interactions with them, our relationships can improve, and we can begin to live more harmoniously with them.

Perhaps, the most valuable thing comparison can bring us, however, is an understanding that it is often a side effect of trying to better ourselves, the irony being that it can also be our downfall on this quest.

How comparison can hurt us

The negative effects of comparison are many and include the following:

- It has a similar impact on the body to physical pain. Indeed, when we experience social pain (such as comparison), our perception and experience of physical pain is heightened.[2]
- It can all too often lead to feelings of resentment towards the object of our comparison when we somehow feel we don't measure up to them.
- The more we compare ourselves to others, the more we weave a story that we are not enough. This story, although fictional, is highly believable and it distorts our capacity to see our true reality, hugely denting our self-esteem.
- Comparing ourselves to others causes us to lose sight of our own goals and aims. Although our quest is to become calmer parents, we become preoccupied with being more like the objects of our comparison, rather than a better version of ourselves.
- Regardless of how well we have done, comparison makes us view our own achievements as unworthy and not good enough if we perceive others to have achieved more than us.
- Comparison makes us more defensive and more likely to lie or twist the truth to live up to the lives of others.[3]
- We undermine our own best characteristics, shrinking to a smaller version of ourselves in the face of the larger-than-life object of our comparison.

- We can succumb to increased levels of perfectionism, especially if we set unrealistic and unachievable goals, based on our perception of others.
- When we focus on how others feel and compare our own feelings to theirs, using them as some sort of gauge for what we should and shouldn't be feeling, we can reduce the validity of what we are experiencing.
- When we compare ourselves to others, we either believe that we are better or worse than them; it is highly unlikely that we will deem ourselves an equal. This perceived superiority or inferiority can lead to disconnect, driving a wedge in relationships and friendships.
- In an attempt to focus on gratitude, if we perceive that we are better off than the object of our comparison, we can experience something known as toxic positivity – the self-imposed pressure to always be happy and positive with our lot, no matter how hard it is, in the mistaken belief that we should always be grateful because somebody is worse off than us. Toxic positivity causes us to repress our own feelings and hide our emotions, suffer painful levels of guilt and stop our enjoyment of life. It can also make us less empathic towards others who are also going through difficult times, but who we perceive to be better off than the original object of our comparison.

Of course, the negative impacts of comparison are also rooted in our present experience. If we are at a time when life is full of difficulty and stressors and we fall into the comparison trap, it can have a further knock-on impact on our self-esteem and confidence. This is compounded if we feel unable to make any constructive change because of our present situation. The phrase 'kick someone when they're down' springs to mind here, although it is even more painful when the kicking is self-inflicted.

Social comparison theory

In the 1950s, psychologist Leon Festinger introduced to the world his social comparison theory.[4] Festinger believed that we all have an in inbuilt, natural drive to compare ourselves with others to provide some sort of a benchmark, by which we can evaluate ourselves, our skills and our abilities.

Social comparison theory identifies two specific types of comparison: upward and downward:

- **Upward comparison** This occurs when we look to others who we presume are better than us in some way. The innate desire here is for a role model and inspiration to help us to improve.
- **Downward comparison** This happens when we look to those we perceive as doing worse than us in some way in a subconscious attempt to feel better about our own situation or abilities.

Children are more likely to engage in downward comparisons than adults. How many times have you heard your child say, 'Well, at least I'm better than x'? Adults, however, tend to engage in more upward comparisons, at least for the first half of adulthood. As we age, we tend to engage less in social comparison and, instead, the object of our comparison becomes our younger selves – something known as temporal comparison; this is arguably the healthiest type of comparison, as it is the one most likely to lead to personal growth and self-improvement, although, understandably, it can lead to regret and lamenting about past abilities lost during the natural ageing process, too.

As parents, we tend to assimilate comparison of our children in the same way as we do comparison of ourselves.[5] Being a parent therefore makes the comparison burden far heavier, because we're not just focused on ourselves but comparison of our children, too.

In addition, the more similar we perceive the object of our comparison to be to ourselves, the harder it is for us. For instance, if we look at the social media profile of a hyper-rich parent with a team of nannies, cleaners, chefs and so on, who appears to be calm and happy with their children all the time, we are less likely to take the comparison to heart than if we considered a neighbour who works the same hours as us and has children of the same age. We can dismiss the rich celebrity parent and explain away their calmness due to the privileges they enjoy, but it is far harder to write off our view of somebody who is our social contemporary.

As mentioned previously, comparison, particularly of the downwards type, is linked with toxic positivity and the two can very quickly become a subconscious race for difficulty, to see who has things the hardest and who is coping the least, or best. If we are struggling and know of others in a similar difficult situation who appear to be coping well, we can also believe that we should be managing better than we are. Comparison weaves a web of deceit, though, and once again, we are comparing our messy tapestry backs to the museum-facing perfect fronts of others. We simply can't win the comparison game.

Social media: the curse of the parent influencer

When I had my first child, the internet was still in its infancy. Social media sites didn't really exist. I often wonder if my parenting experience would have been significantly different if it had started two decades later.

I can see how social media benefits parents. The instant

information and peer advice on tap. The communities and networks that go a long way to replace the lack of in-person support. The adult socialisation and conversation that you so often yearn for in the claustrophobic early months. Social media has a dark underbelly, though. For all that it offers to new parents, it is matched by more sinister, damaging aspects, the worst of these surely being the constant comparison temptation. We are bombarded with images and descriptions of family lives that seem more together, more harmonious, more interesting, more loving, more exciting and, frankly, easier than our own.

But what impact does this have? It undermines everything we have and everything we have achieved. Ours are the gritty real-life documentaries, compared to the fairy tales spun by parenting influencers, paid to present a picture-perfect façade of family life. Social media leaves us questioning everything about our parenting and other aspects of our lives. We're not good enough. We're not fun enough. We're not rich enough. We're not thin enough. We're not fit enough. Our homes are not beautiful enough. We don't take our children on holiday enough. Our social circle is not big enough, or cool enough. Our relationship isn't spontaneous or demonstrative enough. We are not enough. The irony is, however, that everybody feels the same – even (and especially) the parenting influencers. Social media and marketing firms prey on our insecurities and we are all as bad as each other, we just don't realise it.

Research has shown that when we use social media sites, we compare our social lives to those who are social butterflies and as a result, we believe that we have fewer friends and invites than the norm.[6] But here again, we're not comparing like with like. This is a war we will never win, especially if we don't even start on a level playing field. We have always compared ourselves with others, but this has surely increased exponentially over the last decade or two, since the advent of social media. Everywhere we look is the temptation of comparison. On reflection, I am glad I learned how to become a parent in an era when the internet was accessed by painfully slow plug-in dial-up connections, when mobile phones only allowed you to make a phone call or send a basic text and when Mark Zuckerberg was still in high school. I'm not entirely sure I would be here, writing parenting advice books, if I hadn't. More likely, I would have been engulfed in a quagmire of comparison, unable to recognise my own strengths, stuck in a cycle of comparing myself with others.

How to manage comparison

Managing your tendency to compare yourself with others is an important step towards becoming a calmer parent. If you are constantly judging yourself and your children against other families, you will live in a heightened state of stress and an illusionary state, whereby your self-inflicted emotional pain will never leave you feeling good enough. This stress and damage to self-esteem can absolutely impact on your everyday demeanour with your children and your relationships with others.

So how do you beat the comparison curse? I think the first step is acknowledging that you will never be able to stop comparing yourself to others. Trying to do so is utterly futile. Instead, it's about being more mindful of comparison and making it work for you. How can you do this? The following exercises can help:

EXERCISE 1: What can you learn from the objects of your comparison?

Instead of feeling bad that you don't measure up to the objects of your comparison, especially other parents, ask yourself: 'What can I learn from this person?' Research has found that when comparing themselves to others, those who think, 'This person has a view on an issue that I'm dealing with' are happier and calmer than those who think, 'This person is better able to achieve the task than I am.'[7]

The next time you feel the familiar doubts of comparison crossing your mind, pause and ask yourself, *'Is there anything they are doing with their children that I would like to emulate with my own?'* Is there anything you can use in your own parenting to help you, rather than make you feel inadequate. Is there a certain activity you feel may work for your children? For example, perhaps a certain way of organising a specific part of their home that would suit your family?

EXERCISE 2: Make interactions with others more conscious

When we speak to other parents, we tend to 'storytell' ourselves. By this I mean that we don't just observe what is happening or listen to their actual words. We tend to accompany the interaction with internal dialogue, attributing meaning and weight that often don't exist. For instance, if we are talking to another parent about our child's tantrums, they may say, 'Oh yes, it's a tricky age, isn't it, but it isn't too bad.' This means they are admitting that their child does tantrum and that they are finding this stage difficult, albeit something they can cope with. We may, however, perceive them to be brushing off any concerns and saying that their child is always well behaved and that they never struggle. This isn't because of what they said but because we are adding our own feelings and comparison into the mix and somehow turning their words into a slight on our parenting abilities. The next time you have a conversation with a fellow parent, try to really listen to what they actually say, without adding any of your internal dialogue.

EXERCISE 3: Practise acceptance

Everybody compares themselves to others. I started this chapter with the fact that we spend more than a tenth of an average day engaged in comparison. We must accept that these are common thoughts that everybody experiences daily and while we can't chase away comparison, we can learn to live with it as a normal part of everyday life. This acceptance helps us to acknowledge moments of comparison and to embrace them more mindfully before they can do lasting damage to our psyches. We need to forgive ourselves for unnecessarily measuring ourselves against others, especially when it comes to parenting. The next time you find yourself doing this, accept your thoughts for what they are: subjective and likely an inaccurate representation of yourself and others. Once we allow ourselves to experience feelings of comparison without judging them, or ourselves, we can start to recognise that comparison is a misguided attempt to be a better parent.

EXERCISE 4: Correct your erroneous beliefs

We should all focus on believing that we are good parents, not just when it comes to comparison but in every element of parenting. The erroneous beliefs that we form because of comparison can cause so much pain and heartache, and nobody judges us more harshly than ourselves. Spend some time thinking about traits that you feel aren't good enough, based on comparison with others (for instance, 'I am not calm enough', 'I am not playful enough' and so on) and ask yourself if these beliefs are really true or if they've been formed through comparison, by judging your messy tapestry against the inspiring veneer of other parents' museum-facing fronts? Separating fact from fiction and comparison from reality is an important step towards becoming a calmer parent – because if you focus on being a bad, or rather uncalm, parent through comparison, you are likely to believe yourself, and beliefs have a way of spilling through into reality.

EXERCISE 5: Embrace your uniqueness

Imagine if we were all the same. If we all raised our children in identical ways. If we all did the same activities, owned the same items, went to the same places, had the same conversations with our children. What a boring world that would be. We are incomparable, as are our children. We are unique. Embracing our uniqueness as parents is about acknowledging that the inspiring light that we so admire in others sparkles in us, too. Can you spend some time thinking about the positive ways in which others see you? What light of yours do they value? What unique attributes do they admire? Try to see yourself as others see you, and acknowledge your wonderful, unique parenting attributes.

EXERCISE 6: Choose who you spend time with

Do you have a parent friend or acquaintance who brings out the worst in your comparison tendencies? Think about it. Maybe the mum from playgroup or the dad from the football team who always leave you doubting yourself and your children after spending time with them. Maybe they leave you feeling inadequate because they subtly put you down, or maybe they like to gossip about other parents, which makes you wonder what they say about you. You deserve peace. If that peace comes from distancing yourself from competitive friends and acquaintances, then be selective over who you spend your time – and your thoughts – with.

In brief

Before we close, I want to recap on the most pertinent points about comparison:

- Everybody compares. In fact, we spend almost as much time comparing ourselves to others as we do thinking about food. Comparison is, sadly, a fact of daily life. We will never rid ourselves of it, but we can recognise the feelings and manage them more mindfully and positively.
- We compare our insides with the outsides of others. They can never be matched because we don't have the subjective experiences of another's life. We compare the back of our tapestries to the perfect fronts of theirs.
- Downwards comparison can cause toxic positivity; the feeling that we should always be grateful as our lives are not as bad as somebody else's. This causes us to repress our feelings and reduce the validity of our own experience. Just because somebody else is worse off than you, it doesn't mean you're selfish or ungrateful to be struggling.
- When we compare ourselves to others on the internet, we don't play fair. We subconsciously choose to compare ourselves to those who have easier lives than us, and it's a comparison that will always see us lose.
- Ideally, the only person you should compare yourself to is a past version of yourself, to see how far you have come. Self-comparison in this manner can be a good tool for personal growth.
- Comparing ourselves with other parents is a major obstacle in our route to calm parenting because the more we do it, the more we feel resentment, anger, frustration and stress, and the more we feel like this, the more likely we are to lose

our tempers with our children. It is a cycle we must try hard to break if we want to be calmer.

Comparison is something I have worked on a lot with myself over the years. I still feel the familiar creeping anxiety and nagging sensation of self-doubt that it brings when it sneaks in, like an unwelcome but familiar visitor. Now, though, I'm much more adept at recognising it and learning when a thought process doesn't serve me. Ultimately, my family and I are unique, as are you and yours. I'm always reminded of the saying: 'Don't compare your life to others'. There's no comparison between the sun and the moon. They shine when it's their time.' (Author unknown.)

I hope that you have found this chapter helpful, and that it can help you to see and appreciate your own glorious light. Because you can be a calm parent. Calmness isn't something that's in short supply – just like light, there isn't less for you because somebody else's source is burning brightly. There is more than enough to go around.

Chapter 4

The Mental and Physical Load of Parenting – and Why We Must Get Better at Sharing It

We don't have to do all of it alone. We were
never meant to.
      Brene Brown, researcher and storyteller

How many times have you said, 'I just can't take any more', 'I've had it up to here with being a parent!' or, 'I literally don't have the capacity to handle this' – or something similar? Every parent knows how it feels to be emotionally and physically wrung out, exhausted and unable to handle their children. We all know how it feels to be desperate for a break – and by a break I don't just mean a brief week or two in the sun, but real, tangible time away from the demands of everyday life (including our children!). I genuinely believe that parenting would be a whole lot easier if we could only admit how bloody hard it is, and how desperate we are to have some respite now and again. Just because we may struggle with our lives and the demands placed upon us, though, it doesn't mean we hate our children and it definitely doesn't make us horrible people. It makes us real people, with real needs and real limits to what we can handle at any one time. Parenting is tough, and with everything else life throws at us it can sometimes feel impossible. We must acknowledge this before we can attempt to make things easier.

While the physical toll of parenting is without doubt exhausting, I personally find the mental load far more of a drain. We get to switch our bodies off for several hours at night, when we lay still in bed, or collapse on the sofa once all the children are asleep, but our minds continue whirring. Whether we're dreaming about next week's dinner menu or frantically planning a last-minute World Book Day costume, once we become parents it gets harder and harder to switch off our thoughts. The cruel dichotomy of Mother Nature is such that the more time we allow our bodies to be still and rest, the more space we give our minds to run marathons around our heads. As we grow up, the free and fanciful daydreams of childhood become quickly replaced by the responsibility and demands of adulting. Parenting is adulting and then some, though, because we're not only thinking for ourselves, but also have the mental burden of thinking for our children – and often our partners – too.

What happens to us when we carry too much of this mental burden, alongside the very real physical demands of parenting, particularly younger children? We break. We snap. We scream, we shout, we cry. We become the antithesis of calm parents.

The irony here is that usually, it is our very attempts to be such good parents – to 'do it all' for our families – that lead to our demise. Therein lies the problem: to be calmer parents, we must learn to share the load and to carry less. To entrust some of the all-important parenting jobs to others and, sometimes, to ask for help if it is not offered. Doing everything alone, or rather attempting to, doesn't make us *better* parents, but it certainly makes us far less calm parents.

Parental burnout

In 1974, German psychologist Herbert Freudenberger first introduced the term 'burnout'. His work was focused on those who worked in so-called 'helping professions', such as healthcare. The parallels with the helping professions and parenting are many, though. Freundenberger classified burnout as a loss of motivation for the role and tasks at hand, emotional depletion and cynicism towards the role, often resulting in a level of depersonalisation (where you become detached from yourself, your body or your feelings) or an emotional separation from the work. Men are said to tend towards cynicism and depersonalisation when they are overwhelmed and facing burnout; in the case of parenting, these would look like a separation in emotional attachment to the children and their behaviour and needs. Women, on the other hand, are more likely to tend towards emotional depletion and exhaustion, which can leave them feeling drained, tired and unable to cope with their children, or with their role as a mother.

In 1976, Christina Maslach, a professor of social psychology at the University of California, Berkeley, published a scientific paper entitled 'Burned-Out'.[1] This article had a huge impact, cementing the concept as an important area of future research and interest, both among the scientific community and the general public. In the 1980s, Maslach developed a tool to be used by professionals to assess levels of burnout, the key point being that it occurs when the demands of a role or a job are greater than a person's ability to cope with any accompanying stress that it brings.

Physical burnout – the deep-seated exhaustion that accompanies sleepless nights and the relentless physical toil of parenting, particularly in the early months – can be highly damaging, particularly when it comes to the physical toll on the body and relationship to illness and immunity. But emotional burnout can be even more damaging when it results in cynicism and connection problems with our children. Most importantly, however, at least when it comes to this book, emotional exhaustion is a major culprit behind parents' inability to control their tempers and emotions around their children. If we are at rock bottom emotionally, it takes very little to trigger an explosion in us. Emotional burnout is the dark side of the selflessness, self-sacrifice and devotion to their children so common among parents, particularly those inspired by a more gentle, respectful style.

What is the answer to parental burnout? Let's start with what isn't. Relaxation techniques are not going to resolve it, as the common stressors remain and therefore so does the stress response. While job-related burnout can sometimes be resolved simply by leaving the role, this is clearly not an option in parenting. This is why I didn't write this book with a focus on mindfulness, self-care and breathing techniques, as so many parenting or self-help books do. These can all be helpful tools, but often they are superficial and the deeper issues are not discovered and resolved. To reduce burnout, we must work with the root cause and learn to lighten the load a little.

Unequal task division

Research has found that regardless of work outside of the home, women still do more household chores than men.[2] Women are also significantly more likely to remind their partners about outstanding chores than men,[3] so that even if they're not actually completing the work themselves, they are still having to devote headspace to it. Studies have found that conversely, same-sex couples experience a much more equal division of household chores, free of the gender stereotypes that persist through heterosexual relationships.[4] Interestingly, this equality starts to wane a little when they become parents, though, with gay and lesbian couples more likely to adopt a more unequal division of parental responsibilities when children arrive on the scene.[5] If one partner earns more, or works more than the other, a role historically attributed to men, they tend to take on fewer childcare-related chores and responsibilities than their partner, regardless of gender. This unequal division of household and parental tasks is the cause of many problems and disagreements in relationships and also contributes towards struggles with regulating our own emotions as parents.

If you resent your partner, and the fact that you do more chores than them or take on far more of the emotional toil of parenting, this will eventually spill over as resentment towards parenting and, most importantly, towards your children. Combine this resentment with burnout and you have the perfect recipe for anger and emotional outbursts, not only towards your partner, but your children, too.

What parents say

When I spoke with parents, by far the most commonly mentioned obstacle to being calm was that of 'the mental and physical load', especially relating to how it is shared with partners. Here's what some of them had to say:

> I feel like I never have time to relax and properly enjoy time with my children because there's just so much that needs to be done – it makes me feel angry when they ask me to play with them. I feel a lot of guilt when I say no because I've got so much to do and if I don't get everything done daily, it gets out of control and overwhelming to catch up on.

> When I am feeling frustrated with my partner for not helping me, I know deep down that I take it out on the children

rather than confronting my partner. Usually with an outburst like shouting at them.

I get incredibly triggered when I feel like a walking encyclopaedia for our child; everyone asks me, 'Why is he crying?' 'Why isn't he sleeping?' 'Why is he angry?' It's so overwhelming. Especially when coupled with the invisible load of responsibilities that nobody else considers.

The point when I have to think about getting the tea cooked, trying to decide what to prepare, wrestling with the bags in the freezer, entertaining a five-year-old, keeping a twenty-month-old safe – it gets overwhelming. That's when the anxiety builds, then the resentment towards my husband and I begin to lose control.

During demanding, busy periods – Christmas, Easter, the run-up to a holiday, etc. – we are all busy, there's added preparation stress and I'm much less patient than usual!

I get triggered when the dirty dishes are still left from the night before and I'm still expected to sort the child for school, get myself sorted for work and feed the animals while the husband just sorts himself out.

I feel like the weight of the world is on top of me when I'm working, cleaning, doing mum admin and trying to do my best. I get so overwhelmed. I know it's my own mental challenges, trying to be a martyr and do it all, but I hate who it makes me.

I feel like I'm the only one doing everything in the evening. When does my 'work' day end? It doesn't. And I keep going, even when I've used up all in my reserve tank – because until all of the children are in bed I can't stop.

… when I am holding my six-month-old, answering my five-year-old's continuous questions, making the bed and wearing my AirPods waiting for a work call. All at the same time. And my husband looks at me and complains how tired he is. I feel I am about to explode at all of them.

It's the inequality, whether it's the mental load of 'managing the household' or the fact that when our son wakes in the night or is upset, he only wants me. We've had to isolate a lot and while we both work from home, it always seems to be me who has to work and parent at the same time – I feel like I'm spinning so many plates none of them are spinning well.

I struggle with not feeling heard about the little things. Really little, like 'please empty the dishwasher before you clean the rest of the kitchen', then walking in to a still full dishwasher and all the dishes on the sides. Clean, but not away.

I can't cope with mess and the fact that nobody else seems to care about it. We live in a tiny house with little storage. Stuff is everywhere. But apparently no one else can see the mess apart from me!

I struggle with the imbalance of the invisible load between me and my partner. The list of jobs is always a million miles long and only I seem to worry about them.

Parenting job share: Towards a more equal division of labour

You may believe that I am advocating for all families, at least those with two parents in the home, to split all chores, both physical and emotional, fifty-fifty. I am not. This isn't about dividing every element of parenting and household mainten- ance in half, rather, it is about each partner being happy with how the jobs are divided. If one partner is able – and happy – to shoulder 70 per cent of the load, or even more, then that's OK. The problem is when one parent is deeply unhappy with the division of labour or not coping well with it. Maybe they are not consciously aware of the burden they are shouldering and maybe they do not consciously have feelings of resentment towards their partner, but their burnout or temper say otherwise.

My aim with the remainder of this chapter is to help you consider your lot and your comfort with it, and to consider your partner, if you have one, and whether they are happy with the division of both parental and household tasks in your family. Perhaps until now, you have assumed that your partner is OK with how things are shared. Very often families slip into spe- cific roles without any conscious decision being made, but the key to becoming a calmer parent is to have more conversations and make fewer assumptions. Now is the time to think about whether the way you have always done things is the way you should continue in the future.

The place to start, I think, is putting down on paper the tasks you both take on regularly. Very often, we're not truly aware of what our partner or, indeed, we are doing until we see the jobs written down in front of us. This exercise will help you to do just that. Once you have completed the list (you can either just add a tick next to the job that you do or you can add a few words if you feel you want to clarify or expand), and then passed it to your partner to do the same, it's time to have that all-important con- versation. Are you both happy with the division of responsibilities in your family or do you feel that things could be better allocated in a way that would help you to be a happier, calmer parent?

Note: I have left some empty rows at the end of this list for you to add anything else that you think of.

Job	Me	Partner/ co- parent	Other
Meal planning (Deciding on menus for the week, including variations for children based on likes and dislikes and special dietary requirements and researching new recipes, mindful of nutritional needs and preferences)			
Food preparation (Preparing and cooking food for the family and cleaning up after cooking/the food has been eaten)			
Grocery shopping (Stock-taking items already in the kitchen, keeping track of use-by dates, online ordering of new groceries, collecting orders, visiting the store or market, unpacking the groceries and organising storage cupboards, etc.)			
Housework/cleaning (Vacuuming, washing dishes/loading and unloading the dishwasher, dusting, cleaning bathrooms, changing, washing and ironing clothing and laundering bed linen and deeper cleans when required, etc.)			

Job	Me	Partner/ co-parent	Other
Pet care (Feeding, bathing/grooming, cleaning up messes, walking, booking vaccinations, keeping flea/ worm treatments up to date, etc.)			
Managing household finances (Balancing bank accounts, paying bills, switching suppliers/renewing insurances/looking for better deals, speaking to the bank, budgeting for future spends, etc.)			
Liaising with nursery/school (Researching and choosing nursery/school and applying for places, booking and attending parents' evenings, reading and replying to reports, dealing with any problems and concerns arising, etc.)			
Nursery/school events (Organising costumes for plays and special days, taking in donations for fundraising activities, organising teacher presents and cards, completing agreements and permissions and organising payment for trips)			

Job	Me	Partner/ co- parent	Other
Organising clothing for children (Making sure they have the right size shoes and clothing, season appropriate clothing, back-to-school clothing and footwear, organising clothing for special events)			
Gifting organisation (Remembering special dates, planning presents and cards for children, family members, friends and others, shopping for said presents to a budget, sourcing good deals, keeping track of items wanted by children and current likes and interests, wrapping presents and writing cards, posting cards and presents, if needed)			
Family medical needs (Making sure children are up to date with eye tests, hearing tests, nit/worm treatment, routine vaccination appointment making and attendance, keeping the family first-aid kit in good order, treating scrapes and cuts and minor illnesses, booking and attending doctor and hospital appointments, care of children when they're sick and home from school/nursery)			

Job	Me	Partner/co-parent	Other
Holiday planning (Researching family holiday destinations, budgeting/looking for the best deal, organising date availability, booking, and managing payments, organising, and booking holiday activities, ordering foreign currency, checking passports and visas are up to date, purchasing sun cream and beach or pool toys, arranging pet care while away, organising transport to and from the airport or holiday accommodation, planning and packing freshly laundered clothing to take, unpacking, and washing clothing on return from holiday)			
Home and garden maintenance (Keeping everything in safe working order, planning and budgeting for redecorating, choosing new/replacement items, repairing or replacing broken items, lawn mowing and weeding, awareness of changing needs of children regarding furniture and other home items)			

Job	Me	Partner/ co- parent	Other
Car and other transport arrangements (Including charging or filling with fuel, arranging servicing, MOTs, insurance, cleaning, organising bus or train passes and tickets, booking hire cars or taxis)			
Family and friend relationships (Keeping in touch with family and friends, remembering to congratulate for special events or ask after them in times of difficulty, arranging meet-ups, updating them on your own family)			
Researching parenting (Keeping up to date on what to expect of your children's age/stage, learning how to help them with tricky situations and important milestones – for instance, improving sleep or behaviour, potty training, puberty, exams, helping with homework, navigating friendship issues, helping children to develop their reading, writing, drawing and other skills, awareness of any special needs they may have and when they may need more input and support from you)			

Job	Me	Partner/ co- parent	Other
Family entertainment (Planning and organising weekends, days out, school holidays and attendance at special events, such as parties and other celebrations)			
Recording memories (Taking photos and videos of special days and childhood milestones, keeping a baby-record book, writing a diary for your children)			

What if you're flying solo?

I am very aware that so far this chapter has featured a huge amount of privilege in assuming that everybody gets to parent as part of a couple. Of course, this isn't the case. According to official statistics, there are almost 3 million single parents in the UK, accounting for almost 15 per cent of all families.[6] In the USA, this figure is almost double, at around 27 per cent.[7] Some single parents may have the full support of a co-parent within an amicable relationship, while others have a fractious, or toxic relationship, making co-parenting far more difficult. Some may have come to single parenting through choice, while others may have lost their partner through bereavement. Family make-up is unique, but the one thing all parents have in common is that none of them is immune to burnout.

What parents say

I spoke to some single parents and asked them what they struggle with the most. Here are some of their answers:

> The tipping point into overwhelm from the mental load and emotional toll of single parenting. It's not one thing, but a cumulative effect of too much juggling.

> Being a single parent leaves me feeling overwhelmed – physically, emotionally and mentally.

> I'd say a trigger for me is seeing others have a good support network or telling me to 'just ask if you need anything!' – because I spent a lot of my life being shamed for needing help.

I struggle to be a calm parent when I'm overwhelmed from trying to do it all – and trying to do it perfectly. Learning how to let go of my idea of perfection and aim for being 'good enough' has helped me immeasurably; it has shifted my whole experience of parenting.

If you do co-parent with somebody you have an amicable relationship with, then I would strongly suggest that you complete the table on pages 83–88 with them. Even though you may not live together, the division of parenting jobs – particularly those that influence the mental load – is still something that should be discussed. Communication is just as important as if you were living together – perhaps even more so.

If you do not have a relationship with your child's other parent, or they are no longer around or, indeed, were never in the picture, then consider other adults who play a role in your child's life, such as grandparents, aunts and uncles and those who provide childcare. Is there any possibility of speaking to these individuals to see if there are any responsibilities that they can take on to ease your burden a little? I find that those who parent alone are often so focused on doing everything and being proud of their accomplishments (and rightly so!) that they tend to view asking for help as a sign of weakness or an admission that they cannot cope alone. Looking for ways to spread parental chores and tasks around other trusted adults, however, is an important step towards calmer parenting.

How to lighten the load a little

I don't think there is a single parent in the world who cannot identify with the concept of burnout. Parenting is relentless. It's perhaps the only job in the world that you cannot take a sabbatical from, or even sick leave. However tough we are finding things, there are still mouths that need feeding and hands that need holding. So what can you do if you are feel that burnout is inhibiting your ability to stay calm? Give the following a try:

Burnout awareness

The first step towards reducing the impact of burnout on your parenting is being aware of it. Everybody will experience early warning signs before the glaring siren announcing that it has arrived. If we can learn to notice the signs that we are doing too much, we can put safety measures in, hopefully early enough to prevent full-on burnout from happening. The signs are different for everybody, but can include:

- Feeling more tired than normal
- Feeling more short-tempered than normal
- Not wanting to be near your children as much as normal
- Disillusion with parenting and any methods you are trying to follow
- Feeling as if you are a useless parent
- Feeling defeated by parenting, or your children
- Feeling more cynical towards your children, or parenting, than usual
- Feeling trapped and unable to change your situation
- Feeling mentally drained
- Lacking motivation to do things with your children

Learning what your typical burnout symptoms are and recognising them at an early-onset stage allows you to act before they reach a critical level.

Be honest with yourself

Parents often find it difficult to be honest when they have a new baby and a friend or relative asks, 'How are you getting on?' Our instinctive reaction is to reply, 'Everything is great thanks!', even though we may be on our knees with exhaustion. Right from the very beginning of parenting we lie to others about how we're coping. Worse than this, though, we lie to ourselves. We try to convince ourselves that we're doing OK, that we're coping, even when we're not. In fact, especially when we're not. If we can't even be honest with ourselves when we're struggling, how can we ever ask others for help? We must start by having frank and honest conversations in our own heads. Ask yourself the following:

- Realistically how much can you cope with doing in a day/week?
- If you have a partner, or co-parent, do you feel you are carrying an equal load?
- Do you feel resentment (towards another adult, or your children) over the load you are carrying?
- Do you admit to yourself when you're feeling burned-out?
- Do you say 'I can't do any more' often enough?

Recognising, and honouring, our own limits is a sign of strength, not weakness, and it is vitally important if we want to be a calm parent.

Ask for help

Most adults are shockingly bad at asking for help. I believe the cause of this is two-fold. First, we were raised in an era where nurturance and attachment were shunned in favour of forcing early independence and self-reliance. When we had problems in childhood and our difficult behaviour was a disguised cry for help, we were punished by exclusion – we were sent to our rooms, sent out of the classroom, or left to stand in the corner of the room alone. We were taught that if we were struggling, we should keep those emotions inside. Then, as adults, we are bombarded with messages about resilience, grit, perseverance and success. Mental health is still not spoken about enough, or honestly enough, and we subconsciously believe that asking for help is a sign of weakness. These beliefs are of course erroneous, but they are embedded in our psyche and so when we struggle, not only do we struggle with the tasks and chores leading us to burnout, we also struggle with our internal belief that somehow asking for help is inferior to soldiering on alone. Add to this those childhood experiences of feeling shunned, dismissed or let down and it's no wonder that so many of us are reluctant to say, 'I'm not coping, please help!', even to those we love the most. Despite this, however, we must learn to overcome our inner whisperings and realise that saying 'help!' is one of the most important things we can do as a parent.

Prioritise your spinning plates

I often think of parenting as being a circus act. There you are, standing in the centre of a big top, with an audience surrounding you, watching you spin plates on long wooden sticks. Some look on in awe as you carefully balance a multitude of plates, maybe they don't notice as they begin to wobble, or they're looking away when one falls for a split second and you quickly pick it up again, carrying on with your act, before they can emerge from their popcorn. Although life may feel like a series of plates that need to be spun and carefully balanced, we don't need to do all the spinning alone, or indeed to spin as many plates at one time – simply keeping one singular one in the air is impressive enough!

What plates do you have that can be put on an automatic turntable? Left without attention temporarily, while you focus on those more in need of your balancing skills? What plates can be handed to others for safe keeping? What plates are you spinning currently that don't really need to be spun right now? Can you put them down to give yourself a little rest, a brief interlude? Even the best circus performer cannot spin an indefinite number of plates without dropping some, they too must prioritise and know their own limits. What can you take from this metaphor to your own parenting?

Trust others with tasks

Maybe you are OK with the actual act of asking for help, or perhaps help is freely offered to you, but you struggle to trust others. An inability to let go of some responsibilities and entrust them to others is a curse many parents suffer from. Ask yourself why you are reluctant to accept help and share your physical or mental load with others. Were you let down as a child? Did you learn that you couldn't trust others? Or perhaps you are a perfectionist and fear others won't do as good a job as you? Do you try to do everything for your children because you don't believe you are good enough if you don't? Is it because of comparison? Do you feel guilty for something to do with your children and are trying to overcompensate? If you can identify with not accepting or asking for help because you struggle to let go of some responsibility, then trying to understand why you are this way and slowly working to build up your trust of others is key for overcoming parenting burnout. Similarly, resisting the urge to take over somebody's task, because they aren't doing as good a job as you, is important. It doesn't matter if the task is not done as well as it would be if you did it, if it prevents you from getting burned out.

Ask for recognition

Sometimes we are happy with the division of physical and mental labour in our family, but still feel resentment, not because less help is offered, but because our own efforts are not recognised enough. This lack of recognition can leave us feeling underappreciated and as if our work is not important enough to be noticed, or indeed praised. If you are guilty of getting on with things, but struggle with not feeling seen, then the answer here is simple – you need to make your loved ones aware that while you are happy with your lot, you are not happy with the fact that your work is not actively appreciated. If we worked hard in paid employment and were proud of our efforts but our colleagues and managers didn't stop to notice our work, we would raise it in an appraisal or team meeting. Why don't we do the same in our homes? Feeling undervalued and underappreciated can absolutely be a trigger for burnout, even if the jobs themselves are not weighing you down.

Make headspace for calmer parenting

I started this chapter with quotes about feeling 'full up' and having 'had it up to here with parenting'. Without even realising it, we regularly use metaphors that indicate our emotional capacity to absorb stressors. If we are full to the brim, or overflowing with the demands of life, there is no space to 'hold' our children and their tricky emotions and behaviour. What happens if we engage with our children when our heads are full? Even the slightest little thing triggers an explosive reaction. This isn't about our children, it's about us – and our capacity to deal with stress. If we want to be calmer, we need to make headspace so that we are not always walking around on the brink of erupting.

In the 1960s, an English psychoanalyst named Wilfred Bion introduced the idea of containment. This concept describes the way that children project their big, difficult feelings towards their parent or primary caregiver, who then holds and diffuses the emotions before reflecting them back in a more manageable way for the child. In this way parents can 'hold' space for a child's difficult feelings – those that their brains are not mature enough to manage alone – in order to help the child calm down. It's why I advocate staying calm and supportive during a tantrum or other difficult behaviour. Of course, this isn't always as simple as it sounds, because, as I've outlined above, very often parents get full up, and have no space left to contain their child's emotions. When this happens, the parent not only cannot calm the child but they also make things worse by projecting their own difficult feelings – a parental tantrum you might say.

Understanding the capacity, or limit, of your personal headspace is key to becoming calmer. So too is recognising when you are approaching your limit, and need to offload something to make space.

EXERCISE 1: What's in your cup?

In the illustration opposite, write in the cup the big feelings or stressors you are holding at the moment. Now, are there any that you could potentially take away? Or ask for help with? What can you do to make space in your container today, if you're feeling on the edge of burnout, and also to reduce your stressors in the long term?

The power of a good old moan

In an era full of beautifully illustrated positivity quotes and gratitude challenges, one thing I think we all could do with understanding more is that offloading doesn't mean we're ungrateful for our children. It also doesn't mean we want advice on how to do things differently. It's important to hold space better for parents to just have a good old moan, to pour out their difficult feelings from their full-up cups. We need to embrace the power of a good yell, a long moan, a cathartic scream or a healing sob. Letting out emotions is healthy; keeping them locked up for fear of seeming ungrateful, too negative or 'un-gentle' is hugely problematic.

Find somebody who provides support and comfort for you to be yourself and let out your big emotions – somebody with whom you feel safe enough to entrust them with your blackest feelings.

What if you don't have anybody to talk to, though? Feeling isolated can make burnout worse if you don't feel you have an outlet. Here, there is no easy solution, but I think you must start with being honest with your feelings and encouraging others to open up to you, in the hope that one day they will be able to reciprocate. I would also strongly recommend finding an online support group that chimes with your parenting beliefs – somewhere you can speak about parenting and the daily struggles with like-minded people who won't judge you or tell you to stop moaning. (See Resources, page 233, where I have added links to my own groups.) Failing that, having a good old moan to a house plant, photograph, diary or even your dog or cat (hold the yelling, though!) can still be cathartic.

In brief

Before we move on, let's recap on some of the most pertinent points about burnout:

- Burnout can affect us physically and emotionally. It can make us physically ill, but it can also make us feel detached from our children or our role as a parent, cause us to feel disinterested in family life or lead us to feel drained and emotionally dysregulated.
- The results of burnout often cause us to be triggered by our children and their behaviour far quicker than if we were in a state of physical and emotional homeostasis. It is a major obstacle to being calm.
- We can't escape the main cause of stress when it comes to parenting – our children – but we can be mindful about how we handle it.
- An unequal division of parental chores and responsibility or a lack of recognition for our hard work can lead us to feel resentment towards our partners and our children which, in turn, can make us more likely to be angry and emotionally dysregulated towards them.

- We must learn to recognise early symptoms of burnout and seek help, even when that means learning to trust others and resisting the urge to try to take over tasks from them.
- Thinking of our capacity to hold stressors and tasks as a container is a helpful way to view burnout. What is the limit of your cup? Is it full or overflowing? How can you offload a little to make space for both yourself and your children?

I hope that you found this chapter useful. Burnout is something that's very close to my heart, as it's a state I've found myself in many times. I am anything but a calm parent when I'm burned out. In fact, I become an out-of-control, screaming mess. There have been times when I have even scared myself when my cup is overflowing. I don't have any siblings and my parents died when I was in my early twenties, so my support network is pretty much non-existent. I am prone to taking on far more tasks than I can handle and my tendency towards perfectionism makes it hard for me to trust others to take over. That said, I am a work in progress. I am a lot better at identifying my emotional and physical capacities now, largely thanks to the lessons that cancer and the Covid lockdowns taught me, for which I will be forever grateful.

Recognition of an approaching level of burnout and the ability that gives you to make tangible change to avoid it is truly a blessing and something that has a tremendous impact on your level of peace and calm in every element of daily life, especially parenting. I strongly recommend that all parents focus on this and I will never stop trying to work on it personally. The more space we have, the more able we are to meet whatever parenting throws at us with grace. And this is a good point to end on, with the next chapter focusing on the importance of flexibility and adaptability in parenting.

Chapter 5

Moving with the Tide and Letting Go of Control – How to Tackle Life Transitions with Grace

Dance with the waves, move with the sea.
Let the rhythm of the water set your soul free.

Christy Ann Martine, poet

We are creatures of habit who find comfort in the familiar, particularly in times of stress. We feel at our most safe when life is predictable and we feel in control. We live in a constantly changing world, though – as perfectly illustrated in 2020 when the Covid pandemic hit and everything we knew was turned upside down overnight. This change and the many transitions we face in the course of everyday life can be a huge trigger for us. Just when we feel that we may be becoming calmer parents, something changes. We are faced with new challenges and the need to adapt. And the change needn't be as traumatic as the Covid-19 pandemic, which brought so many parents to their knees with exhaustion and stress from having to be both home educators and home workers overnight, isolated from their usual support sources. Sometimes the small transitions prove just as explosive for us. But no matter the size of the change, the impact on our calmness can be huge.

Change and transitions can leave us feeling unsettled and stressed, and this stress can make it significantly harder to stay calm with our children. In a time of turmoil and change, we seek structure – and when that structure crumbles, so too can our reserves and patience. But as well as the unexpected curveballs life throws at us, like Covid-19, parenting – and our children – don't stay static. Life transitions are unavoidable, and so we must learn to move with the tide of life, surfing the waves of change, rather than battling to keep them at bay. Because although we may be able to hold back change for a short time, our hastily built mental blocks will eventually break down. So what's the answer? Ultimately, to learn to accept life's transitions, both big and small, with grace. It sounds so simple, doesn't it? And it is really, but it's anything but easy to implement.

The metamorphosis of parenting

Pregnancy sees the start of our transition to a new identity, regardless of whether we are male or female. The newborn period isn't only about the birth of a baby, it's about the birth of a parent, too. You were an entirely different person until the moment that you held your child in your arms for the first time. Parenting has a clever way of making you re-evaluate everything in your life. It causes you to examine your beliefs, your actions, your words and your relationships, as well as moving in like a whirlwind and rearranging every practical aspect of your pre-children life. And what do we do in response to this monumental change? We fight it, usually subconsciously. We try to cling to the past and desperately try to add order and predictability to our days.

In the newborn days, we desperately try to follow prescribed sleep schedules and wake windows. We chart our baby's feeds and try to stick to feeding routines; we look to centile charts to see what they should weigh. We pore over books that tell us what our babies should be doing day by day. We focus on prescribed timings for so-called developmental leaps, trying to map, chart and predict our child's behaviour like a weather or astrological forecast. Sometimes this planning and predicting can help us in our transition; other times it can leave us feeling far more stressed and anxious than if we'd just tried to move with the tide or go with the flow.

MATRESCENCE: THE MOTHERHOOD TRANSITION

I've been working with new parents for almost two decades now and have always been fascinated by the transition from child-free to parent. Did you know that there is a word to describe the huge physiological and psychological transition that women make when they become mothers? Coined in 1973 by medical anthropologist Dana Raphael, that word is 'matrescence'. The fact that most people have never heard of this word is a measure of how under-researched, misunderstood and undervalued this tremendous transformation is for new mothers. And this is why they need support, empathy and understanding and time, not unwanted advice and expectations that they should 'get back to normal' (whether that be their pre-baby bodies, their careers or their housekeeping) quickly. The thing is that normal has changed. There is no 'getting back' to anything, because now everything is different for her. Body, mind, heart and soul – she will never be the same again.

Does this apply to only mothers? Of course not. While Raphael's work focused on matrescence, more and more are now speaking of patrescence: the psychological transition that new fathers make after a child arrives, because it isn't only mothers who form a new identity in the postnatal period.

Can you imagine how much easier new parenthood might be if matrescence and patrescence – and the unique challenges they encompass – were spoken of freely in our society? If we acknowledged the tremendous change and transition that new parents have to make, on top of coping with the demands of sleepless nights and chaotic days punctuated with feeds, nappy changes and consoling tears?

The reality of parenting makes us confront the visions and expectations we held – and still hold – of our children, our partners, our friends and family and ourselves. Often our expectations are out of sync with reality, and we can feel confused and let down when the vision clashes with real life. Working as an antenatal teacher, I found that those who had taken a particularly long time to conceive, especially if they had welcomed a child through assisted conception, would often have a more difficult birth and a harder fourth trimester (the first three postnatal months) than those who had conceived quickly and easily. I often wondered if this was due to the extra time they had spent constructing post-baby events and experiences in their minds and the expectations they had of themselves and the ideal motherhood or fatherhood, leading to increased anxiety when things didn't measure up to their dreams. Sometimes it's not the unexpected transitions that we find so difficult, but the ones we have waited years for and dreamed of a thousand times.

The change in need as children grow

Although initially becoming parents is undoubtedly the largest life transition many of us will make, it is by no means the only one we will face as parents.

As our children grow, we desperately try to grasp the control that is slipping away from us. We want predictability and we want instructions, but children don't come with these things, and the more we fight the natural flow of parenting, the harder it becomes. I find one of the hardest parts about raising older children is that they are approaching huge moments of transition in their own lives, such as puberty, moving to secondary school, college or university, starting serious romantic relationships and the like, while my own life is in huge transition as I go through the menopause and I begin to prepare for the next stage of my life and all the emotional turmoil that entails. In many ways, it feels unfair. I often wonder how much easier it would be to raise tweens and teens if I had nothing else to contend with in my life. No hot flushes, no worries about retirement plans and no mid-life regrets or worries. Added to this, many parents will find themselves in something known as 'the sandwich generation'. Those who are raising their own children through huge moments of transition, while also caring for elderly relatives whose needs, both physical and emotional, increase with each passing year. The stress that accompanies being the filling in the needs sandwich, being tightly compressed by each slice of metaphorical bread, can sometimes feel overwhelming, especially when you consider if there is ever time to meet your own needs, too.

How transitions change our behaviour

It is a well-accepted parenting fact that transitions commonly result in difficult behaviour from children. Tantrums, whining, sulking and 'lashing out' or violent behaviour are all common reactions to periods of change for children, especially when they are having to transition from something that they enjoy, or feel comfortable with, to something new and unknown, or something that they know they struggle with or don't want to do. A classic example here would be a child who doesn't want to leave the park, whose disappointment, frustration and dysregulated emotions result in a tantrum with lots of screaming and shouting. Other times of transition that bring heightened emotions and dysregulated behaviour from children include a new sibling arriving in the family and starting preschool or school. If I am consulting with a parent about their child's tricky behaviour, I will always start by asking what transitions that child is going through, and what change they are having to assimilate into their lives.

The dysregulated behaviour I just described obviously focuses on children, but the same applies to adults. Transitions often throw a spanner in the works of calm parenting, just as you think you are starting to have things sorted, bam – something happens and change is afoot. Transitions can leave us feeling disorientated, confused, frustrated and anxious and can trigger in us the same difficult behaviour we see in our children. Parenting books and advice websites – including my own – talk a lot about children grappling with transitions, but far less attention is given to helping parents with theirs. It is assumed that as we are grown adults, we can cope with them. But actually, I think we can struggle just as much as children, if not more so, because often we are not only having to work through our own emotional reactions, but also our children's.

Transitions may be exciting and welcomed, such as a new job, or they may be unexpected or unwelcome, particularly if they come about through traumatic situations, such as Covid-19 or a bereavement. Alterations to daily routines, having to learn new skills, changes in our eating and sleep can all be discombobulating. This is often why we find it difficult to relax when we go on holiday. We arrive desperate to chill out, but all the change can leave us feeling temporarily stressed. It always takes me about a week to relax into a holiday. In the first few days, I inevitably have trouble sleeping and get frustrated with myself at my inability to unwind and switch off my worries about what I've left behind at home. Ironically, the more we consciously try to chill out, the harder we tend to find it. That holiday loosening up usually hits when I stop fretting about my lack of calmness and get caught out in the enjoyment and relaxation, unaware that I have succumbed to it.

Larger transitions challenge our self-identity and can leave us feeling unanchored. They can be a trigger for burnout, perfectionism (as we are constantly analysing our actions and reactions) and comparison (as we compare our abilities to those of others going through a similar transition), and the lack of stability can bring up unresolved issues from our childhoods. At the very least, life transitions can be stressful because, by their very nature, they bring about change, which requires us to work harder to restore a sense of normality and equilibrium.

ANXIETY AND TRANSITIONS

Transitions can be a strong trigger for anxiety, especially in those who are already anxious. Difficult reactions to change are often rooted in fear. That may be a fear of the unknown, fear of failure, fear of being hurt or fear of repeating past mistakes. Whatever the cause, coupled with pre-existing anxiety, it can leave us in a very vulnerable state, and we will often try to avoid the transition or fight against it as a form of self-protection. Transitions make us confront our beliefs, actions, experiences and relationships. All of which can, again, be a huge trigger if we struggle with anxiety or self-esteem issues already.

I include myself here as somebody who has struggled with anxiety for as long as I can remember. In fact, I don't recall a time of my life when I wasn't anxious. My coping mechanism leads me to plan, plan and plan some more and I struggle if my plans need to change direction or become derailed. Acknowledging that you are struggling is the first step here. You must be aware of your thoughts, triggers and typical responses if you are going to try to make change. As the years have passed, I have worked hard on my anxiety during times of transition, and although I am by no means zen, I have become a lot calmer using some of the tips I will share with you later in this chapter.

What counts as a life transition?

It's important to understand that everybody experiences life transitions differently, and what may be a welcome and easy change for some can be incredibly traumatic for others. However, the following are commonly regarded as potentially difficult life transitions:

- Puberty
- Moving house
- Changing jobs or returning to work after parental leave
- Relationship breakdowns
- New relationships starting
- Changes in friendships
- Your child starting day care or school
- Welcoming a new baby into your family
- Children leaving home or starting university
- A change in your health or that of a loved one
- Bereavement
- Menopause
- Retirement.

In Chapter 10, I will talk more about parenting through difficult times and periods of big change and challenge, encompassing several of these points.

Small transitions

Sometimes the most inconsequential transition can cause you the biggest heartache. Something I struggled with the most when I had young children was the difficulty of leaving the house on time. My anxiety had made me very punctual before

I had children – I was always the person who turned up half an hour early to a party or interview, for fear of being late. And if I did arrive late somewhere, which only ever happened through no fault of my own pre-children, I felt terrible. I would apologise profusely, panic and feel incredibly irritated. You can imagine how I coped, then, when I had children. I went from being super punctual to super late overnight, whether because a baby had filled their nappy just as we walked out of the door, a toddler was tantruming about wearing the wrong-colour shoes or a teenager refused to get out of bed on time and then spent an hour in the shower. Being late inevitably turned me into an out-of-control, shouty parent. The distress and dis-ease of being late was soul-destroying in the early years and I took a lot of the resulting difficult feelings out on my children. Ironically, the more I lost my cool, the harder getting out of the house would be as my children picked up on my stress and responded with their own tantrums. A decade or two later and I've now learned to accept being a little bit late. Or rather, I've learned to accept the things that I really can't control. I've also learned that apologising and stressing myself out over my lack of punctuality doesn't serve anybody – because not only do we arrive late, but we also arrive with me with a severely frayed temper, which inevitably means sulky or poorly behaved children, too.

One thing that has really helped me with this particular problem is shifting my focus from apologising to thanking. Instead of constantly saying, 'Sorry we're late', I now say, 'Thanks for waiting for us.' It doesn't change the fact that we didn't arrive on time, but it does change the way you think about it. And I think, perhaps, this is key to coping with small but tricky transitions – not avoiding them, not overly stressing over them, but accepting them and being mindful of how you react.

What do we need in times of transition?

Ultimately, during difficult transitions, we need the same treatment as young children when they're struggling with leaving the park or becoming a new big brother or sister: understanding, compassion, patience and some forward planning – only these are all self-directed, rather than being directed towards our children.

I think the following are the most important to consider when it's we who are dealing with tricky transitions:

- Preparation – drawing up a plan to follow, breaking things into manageable chunks.
- Realistic expectations – just as we shouldn't expect our toddlers to have the emotional-regulation skills of adults, we shouldn't expect ourselves to take to new, especially big transitions like a duck to water. We are going to struggle, we are going to find it difficult, and that's OK.
- Acceptance – change is an inevitable part of life; we can't avoid it, but we can learn to reflect on it.
- Support – finding somebody or a source of information to support you is key, especially if the transition requires a new understanding of something.
- Connection – connecting with others who understand and are happy to 'hold' you, in much the same way that we spoke about containment in the previous chapter, enables you to focus on regulating your own emotions, by mirroring those of the people you are connecting with.
- Self-compassion – just as we would show compassion towards a child struggling with a life transition, we should be kind to ourselves. We must allow ourselves the time and space we need to feel all of our feelings without judgement.

Let's end this chapter with looking at some exercises and activities that can help us to stay calmer in times of transition.

Tips and exercises to help you in times of transition

The following activities can help to lessen the stress, anxiety and, finally, dysregulated and angry parenting outbursts that accompany times of transition. By no means do you have to follow all of them, but I hope that you will find one or two that work for you.

Bullet lists

I love a list. They help me to feel in control of even the most uncontrollable situations. First, making a list provides important headspace time – moments when you can sit and plan through all eventualities and consider what you need to have or do. The act of committing your ideas to paper (or screen) cements the planning you have done and the lists act as a kind of scaffolding to help you feel supported. I'm a fan of written paper lists and also have a blackboard in my kitchen where I regularly jot down things that need to be done. I also keep copious lists on my laptop and phone, as I find they provide me with a lot of reassurance, even if I don't actually stick to them.

EXERCISE 1: Write a daily bullet list

Can you write a bullet list daily for a week? Make a note of anything that you want to accomplish the following day each evening and cross off the actions as you complete them the following day.

Set yourself small, achievable goals

Although reaching for the stars is certainly admirable in terms of ambition, setting our sights much lower is probably more realistic. If we stretch our goals too much, not only can they sometimes feel unachievable but we can also feel guilt, remorse and self-deprecation when we fail to meet them – all of which can significantly disrupt our ability to be a calm parent.

EXERCISE 2: Break it down

The next time you set a goal, break it down into several smaller chunks, so that you can tick each of them off before moving on to the next one, and see how different you feel using that approach.

Daily journaling

Did you keep a diary as a teenager? It's something many of us did but consigned to our memory boxes when the pressures of adulthood took hold. Daily or even weekly journaling can really help to make sense of our feelings, though, especially during times of big transition (which is why so many teens take to them during puberty).

EXERCISE 3: Rediscover journaling

Pick a beautiful new notebook and pen and, when you have time, take just a few minutes to acknowledge and honour your feelings by writing them down. Doing this can provide a surprising amount of support.

EXERCISE 4: Visualising

If you find yourself struggling with a particular transition, sit somewhere quietly, close your eyes and visualise yourself in past times when you have made changes successfully. Imagine that same feeling of achievement with the new challenge and imagine bringing some of the calmness you felt then to what you are facing now.

Ritual and routine

In times of transition, when we feel particularly out of control, rituals and routines can really help us. A good example is a funeral service. The focus on planning flower displays, readings, mourning outfits and the like provide a creative outlet for some of our grief and help with our anxiety at a difficult time. Another example is menarche (the start of menstruation) celebrations. There is an increasing interest in this in Western society, as it can help young girls to process and embrace the changes that are happening to their bodies. If we can add ritual and routine to our transitions, we can lean into them during moments of stress and anxiety.

EXERCISE 5: Create a ritual

If you or your children are struggling with a transition at the moment, can you think of a new family routine, or ritual, that would help you to manage? For example, you could create a ritual around your child starting school. This could be devising a special song to sing when you say goodbye to each other on their first day, or a special family meal the night before they start school. If you are moving house, your ritual may involve saying goodbye to each of the rooms, spraying a scent that is special to you and eating your last meal in a room that holds the most special memories for you, thanking it for being your home; then, in the new house you could repeat the ritual, this time saying 'hello' to each of the rooms, spraying the same special scent in all corners and choosing a space in which to have a special 'moving-in meal'.

EXERCISE 6: Focus on the positives

Transitions can be a time of great learning for us, although it is often hard to appreciate this in times of difficulty and distress. Try to find a few moments of calm and peace where you can focus on any new skills you have acquired, new experiences or possibilities that have opened up or new relationships you have formed because of the transition. Write them down in your journal.

Labyrinth art

When I worked as a doula and antenatal teacher, there was a growing interest in using labyrinths during pregnancy to prepare for birth. The labyrinth was said to represent moments of transition (for example, birth), with U-turns, wrong paths, dead ends, doubling back upon yourself, before finally reaching a clear path to the exit or centre. Visualising a labyrinth can help us to be mindful of our journey, if we are aware of the different twists and turns it can take but understand that these are all part of the process of reaching the end point.

EXERCISE 7: Draw your own labyrinth

Try drawing a simple labyrinth, like the one below, plotting out any transitions you are struggling with, noting the most difficult points, wrong turns and times when you have felt that you are going backwards. This will help you focus on what the journey to your goal will look like. And remember that the end is always in sight, even if it feels like the journey to get there is complicated right now.

GOAL

START

In brief

Before we end this chapter, I thought it would be a good idea to sum up some of the basic points surrounding transitions that we should try to understand and practise in the quest to be calmer parents:

- Parenting involves many transitions, from matrescence and patrescence, all the way through to children flying the nest and leaving home. It is common to struggle with these, but we should be aware that this struggle can have a very negative impact on our ability to be a calm parent.
- Everybody has trouble with transitions, and just as they can bring lots of big difficult feelings and behaviour for children, the same is also true for adults. Our own feelings and behaviour can quickly deteriorate when we are dealing with a transition.
- Small changes can be as difficult as the big life transitions. Don't dismiss their impact – for example: 'I coped with having a baby and moving house in the same year, why am I struggling with starting at a new gym?'
- In much the same way that we would support our children or loved adults we must show ourselves compassion when we are facing transitions, and allow ourselves the same understanding.
- Breaking the change down into smaller, more achievable steps – whether we use bullet point lists, journaling, labyrinth art or similar creative exercises – helps us to stay on track, to form realistic expectations and to make the transition feel more achievable, all while helping us to stay as calm as possible.

I hope that this chapter has helped you to understand the impact of transitions on your life and, importantly, on your ability to be a calm parent. The transitions that parenting in particular brings to us can generate some beautiful metamorphoses if we let them. We just need to approach them mindfully and allow them to gently shape and change us, rather than battling against the oncoming waves. I'll leave you with a quote that always helps me in times of transition, from professor of medicine and mindfulness author Jon Kabat-Zinn: 'You can't stop the waves, but you can learn how to surf.'

Chapter 6

Why Busy Is Not a Badge to Aim For – Discovering the Lost Art of Doing Nothing

Sometimes sitting and doing nothing is the best thing you can do.

Karen Salmansohn, author

When was the last time you sat down and did nothing without feeling guilty? Maybe your baby or toddler was napping, your preschooler engrossed in play, your eight-year-old watching a film or your teen out with their friends and you found yourself unexpectedly free. Free of the demands of childcare, albeit temporarily, with no pressing work assignments and no life admin that needed to be attended to 'right now', you contemplated on the best use of your time. Maybe you sat and enjoyed the peace for a couple of minutes, before your mind soon turned to the housework that needed doing, the meal prepping and shopping list that needed writing, the laundry that needed putting away and the grass that needed mowing. And then you felt that familiar pang of guilt. Guilt over the fact that you shouldn't be taking a break with so much to do. Guilt that it was lazy of you to sit and relax when your house was in such a mess, or because you had invoices to send or emails to answer ...

This guilt, and our inability to be still, in body and mind, instead constantly seeking to cram every waking moment full to the brim with 'stuff', is a curse of modern-day life and a major obstacle to calmer parenting. Because when we fail to slow down and take a breath, we head rapidly for burnout – and burnout results in stress and anger that is inevitably directed at our children.

Our society's pervasive view is that the most successful people are usually the busiest. Ergo, those who do less achieve less. Hard work and busyness are praised. Down time and a slower pace are akin to laziness and lower productivity. This belief is the downfall of many adults, not just parents, but it is simply not the case. Parenting is already busy enough, without the extra demands that life throws at us. We cave under the pressure and, ironically, end up achieving less when we stretch ourselves too thin and push ourselves to our limits and beyond. Being busy doesn't make us successful and it certainly doesn't make us better parents. In fact, the busier we become, the less calm we are with our children. We need to stop glamourising being busy. Doing less isn't lazy or inferior; it's often the smartest choice.

Why rewarding busy is so damaging

In 2012, I won a national competition, sponsored by a large mobile-phone brand, and was crowned 'Britain's Busiest Mum'. As part of my prize package, I spent the day in London, with a full team of stylists, hairdressers, make-up artists and photographers, who primped and preened me for a photoshoot that appeared in a bestselling glossy magazine. A full-page spread announced that I had won the accolade for all the work that I did, raising four children, running my own business in the daytime, writing books and blogging in the evenings and teaching antenatal classes at weekends. I also worked 'on-call' as a birth doula, volunteered on our school parent–teacher association and acted as a committee member of my local pre-school. The magazine write-up praised me for juggling so many balls and achieving so much. In the large close-up picture of my face, I looked glowing, with smooth, shiny hair and beautiful make-up, all topped off with a big smile. My life seemed perfect – aspirational, even. As well as the makeover, I won a two-week Caribbean holiday, which they said was to give me a well-earned rest. What the piece didn't say was how absolutely exhausted I was. How I was so wrung out that even brushing my hair in the morning was so much of a chore for me that I would go for days with it scraped up into a bun, a bird's nest of matting underneath. The tiredness was so extreme I felt permanently ill and my immune system seemed almost non-existent. Life was a cycle of virus after virus and I begged my GP to test me to work out why I was so tired all the time, but blood tests, of course, showed there was nothing wrong medically. My temper was so frayed that I would regularly shout at my children. I spent all day, every day, serving others and had no time for myself. The article was a lie and I look back now and realise how damaging the whole conversation was. Being 'Britain's Busiest Mum' is not something we should aim for, but something we should avoid at all costs. It is a ridiculously destructive concept and one I am deeply sorry I ever became involved with.

The answer is usually less, not more

When we try to think of how to be better at something (for instance being calmer) we tend to think about *what else* we can do – something scientists refer to as 'additive behaviour' – rather than what we can take away. When I announced I was writing this book, I received many messages asking me if I was going to write about the usual 'self-care, yoga, meditation, mindfulness and taking up a hobby' that you find in most self-help books aimed at stressed-out parents. When I replied, 'Actually, no; I'm going to be focusing on the reasons behind *why* we're stressed and seeing what we can remove from the baggage that is preventing us from being calmer,' the response was usually one of surprise.

We live in a culture that constantly tries to make us do more, buy more and be more. The idea of less does not come naturally to us. Science agrees that we're more likely to try to fix a problem by adding something than taking something away.[1] Researchers from the University of Virginia's School of Engineering and Applied Science looked at why we are more likely to attempt to solve a problematic situation by adding things, rather than attempting to take something away, theorising that it was because it requires more cognitive effort to focus on solutions based on subtractions and because we have an unconscious bias to go with our first ideas, which are usually solutions based on addition.

WHAT THE COVID LOCKDOWNS TAUGHT US

One of the most powerful messages that the Covid-19 pandemic taught many of us was the power of doing less. Overnight, the world was thrust into involuntary lockdowns and we were forced to stay at home, many of us unable to work or on furlough from our jobs. Although in many ways the lockdowns tested us to the extreme, especially those with children who found themselves taking on the role of full-time teacher on top of everyday parenting duties, in other ways it provided us with important lessons. We learned that entertainment doesn't always have to happen outside of the home to be of value. We learned the value of simple activities such as baking and vegetable growing, and we learned that spending time walking in the fresh air was more beneficial to us than we ever could have imagined. The lockdowns made us re-evaluate our pre-Covid lives; many of us would never return to the office full-time, with blended home-and-office working – once a distant pipe dream – becoming a reality. Covid taught me to value the little things; to take pleasure in the everyday. And, most of all, it taught me to slow down. After more than a year of a slower pace, I was in no hurry to return to the busy normality of life before Covid and I know I'm not alone.

The power of a regular day of 'doing nothing'

Do you remember the long summer days of your childhood? The days when you had nothing planned, no organised activities and no commitments. You could play in the garden, making mud pies and daisy chains, or roam around the streets with your friends, cycling to each other's houses and talking for hours. Days of 'nothing' turned into some of the best days of our lives. My favourite childhood memories involve Sundays. I am a child of the 1980s and 90s, an era when most shops were closed on a Sunday. (It wasn't until 1994 that trading laws changed and allowed shops to open on Sundays, with restricted hours.) My childhood Sundays were filled with roast dinners, lawn mowing, car washing, fishing, walks, visiting family and sitting in the garden reading the magazines that accompanied the Sunday papers. Most children and teens today would be horrified at such boring weekends, but to me they were blissful. Those days provided all-important down time, connection and essentially forced relaxation. Nowadays, Sundays are no different to any other busy day. We can shop at any time, with 24/7 supermarkets and online shops just a click away. We have entertainment on demand and we rarely embrace the boring normality of spending time at home doing nothing. I think there is a strong argument to take a little bit of the past into the present and honour one day of rest per week again. If a day a week seems too ambitious, then aim for just a couple of hours each week when you focus on doing less and enjoying the simple joys of everyday life.

The power of play
(yes, even for adults)

Do you remember the joy you used to get from drawing and colouring or playing with Lego or Scalextric sets as a child? Play is the primary tool of learning for children and is seen as important and necessary. When we become adults, however, play is seen as frivolous and time-wasting. The play itself never loses its value, however; we just view it differently based on the age of the individual who's doing it.

Play is a truly wonderful tool for helping us to relax and become calmer parents. Many play exercises are perfect illustrations of mindfulness in practice. Play can teach us to slow down, to release pent-up difficult feelings in safety, to focus on the here and now and put our problems aside temporarily. Play is also a truly wonderful way of connecting with our children. Play has never lost its value as we've grown up, regardless of what society may tell us. Learning how to play again, to enjoy colouring in, piecing together puzzles or racing a remote-control car around your living room – not just with your children, but by yourself, too – is a wonderful way to regain some calm in your life. Play is never time wasted, but rather time well invested, and we would all be better parents if we engaged in more of it.

Boundaries: your secret calm-parenting weapon

As I've got older, I've realised the power of saying 'no' more. In my thirties, my self-worth and value of myself as a parent seemed tied to how much I did, particularly for other people. I held an unconscious belief that if I took on as much as possible and helped out as much as I could, people would not only like me more but would also consider me a better mother. I realise now how ridiculous this sounds, but I'm by no means alone in this thinking. People pleasing and an almost inability to say 'no' is a common affliction among parents, particularly mothers. But we don't need to earn respect and admiration from others because we're busy; we're worth just as much when we're relaxing, or when we say, 'No. I'm sorry, I'm at capacity right now.' We should all beware of taking on more than we can realistically handle (especially balanced with parenting and our own needs and mission to become calmer parents) in some mistaken quest to convince ourselves and others that we are capable. Saying 'no' is freeing (an idea we will pick up on again later on when we talk about adult relationships) and allows us to focus on our own needs and journeys to become calmer parents. It's something I have embraced fully over the past couple of years.

HOW TO SAY 'NO' MORE

Saying 'no' seems to be a bit of a social taboo, and so, for fear of sounding rude, we often take on far more than we can handle. I was hugely guilty of this, because I was worried about how others would perceive me if I said 'no', particularly from a professional perspective. My inability to say 'no' cost me dearly, both in terms of my emotional and physical health and my relationship with my children. I knew I had a problem, and so I invested time in observing others I admired and learned how they said 'no' without remorse or any negative comeback from those they were refusing. I now have a few stock phrases that I use, when I feel that old familiar guilt slipping back in and I'm tempted to say 'OK' when my heart and soul are screaming at me to say 'no':

- 'Thank you so much for thinking of me. I'm afraid I'm at capacity right now.'
- 'I would love to help, but I just can't take anything else on right now.'
- 'I wish I could say "yes", but unfortunately I'm too busy.'
- 'I can't help, but I do know somebody who may be able to.'
- 'Unfortunately, this isn't something I could help with, but here's a link/telephone number that may be useful.'
- 'Now isn't a good time for me, but thanks so much for asking.'
- 'I'm sorry I'm unable to do this, but I wish you the best of luck.'
- 'Not right now, I'm afraid, but check in with me again in the future.'

- 'This isn't for me, sorry.'
- 'Gosh, it sounds great, but I've just got too much on, so will have to pass.'

Saying 'no' is definitely something that gets easier the more you practise it. Think of it as a muscle you have to exercise. Initially, it feels really uncomfortable and sometimes painful, but the more you exercise it, the more it builds until, eventually, it feels easy.

Boredom: the best gift you can give your children

Another way parenting guilt can sneak in and make us over-stretch ourselves is with our tendency to want to fill every waking moment of our children's days with entertainment and sensory- or stimulation-rich activities. In short, we are a generation who are afraid of our children getting bored. We micromanage school holidays and weekends. We schedule evenings with military precision, and we worry that we aren't doing enough, especially when our children cry, 'I'm bored.' The pressure so many parents feel to entertain their children is ridiculous.

I want to let you into three valuable parenting secrets:

1. It's OK for your children to be bored. It is in no way a reflection of your parenting ability.

2. It's OK to not plan special activities or entertainment with your children at weekends and during school holidays.

3. Boredom is really good for children.

Having bored children and no plans, aside from the regular routine of daily family life for weeks on end does not make you a bad parent, just as filling every day with theme parks, picnics, soft play, cinema and theatre trips, activity camps, swimming, play dates and the like does not make you a good parent. I'm not saying that there is something wrong with organising special activities with your children if you all enjoy it or if they are necessary as a form of childcare while you work. I am also not attacking those of you who find that getting out of the house and doing stuff with your children, keeping you all occupied, is a way to avoid sibling bickering. Instead, I am simply warning that if you find the constant pressure to entertain your children in your otherwise 'free time' stressful, then it will impact on your ability to be calm – and in this case, reining things in a little is a very wise move.

WHY IS BOREDOM SO GOOD FOR CHILDREN?

Boredom is definitely something we should embrace, rather than desperately try to avoid. Boredom helps children to:

- develop their imaginations
- build resilience
- grow their creativity
- acquire problem-solving skills
- better their relationships.

All of these can help to boost a child's self-esteem and confidence, and they also provide important groundwork for their future adult personalities – because an individual who is happy to be by themselves is one who is likely to experience healthier relationships as they grow.

The simplest memories are often the best

I often hear parents say they feel the need to arrange days out and activities in order to create special memories for their children. This idea, however, completely undermines what parents bring to the table during everyday family life. Children treasure time and connection with their parents, which can happen just as easily (and far more cheaply) at home.

What are some of your own most treasured childhood memories? Do they involve organised activities, clubs and elaborate days out? Or are they more focused on your home and family? When I was a child, my parents organised very few activities for me, or for us as a family, largely because they simply couldn't afford to constantly entertain me with expensive days out or clubs. Instead, I would 'play out' with my friends, make all sorts of concoctions with flowers and mud in our garden, bake fairy cakes with my mum, ride my bike up and down our road, watch an hour or two of children's television (I grew up in an age when that's really as much as there was on an average day!) and wash the car with my dad. Sometimes, on warm days, I would just lie on the grass on a blanket and read a library book for hours on end, draw or write letters to my pen pals. We might have one special-treat day at the end of the holidays and a few picnics in a local wood, but that really was it. I do remember frequently complaining of being bored but, retrospectively, I really value what those days taught me. Perhaps your own childhood was similar? Now, children's days are so full, with many children rushed off their feet, moving from one activity to the next. Both children and parents look exhausted, and we all know what happens to our stress levels when exhaustion sets in.

Getting off the socially acceptable 'organised-activities'

treadmill is something that may work for you in your quest to be calmer. Perhaps the biggest problem with overscheduling and over-entertaining our children is that the more we do with them, the less likely they are to be comfortable with being bored and, of course, the more bored children become, the more likely they are to whine about their boredom and the more likely we are to lose our calm when we respond. It is a self-fulfilling prophecy that often results in stress and exhaustion all around. The only way to break the cycle is to get off it.

Anti–busy challenges and exercises

The path to being 'un-busy' can be a difficult one, because the prevailing culture of doing more means that our lives fill up with 'stuff' and it feels like second nature to us. Doing less involves going against the cultural grain and often breaking cycles from our own upbringings. Try the following exercises to help you to move towards reducing busyness in your life:

EXERCISE 1: Allocate half an hour in your weekly diary to do nothing

If you are not used to relaxing, or having free time in your diary, it's probably not the best idea to jump into devoting half a day a week to doing nothing. Instead, try to build up from small periods of time. Schedule half an hour per week of 'nothing' and work hard to avoid distraction. This is not time to write to-do lists in your head or spontaneously decide to deep clean an area of your home. It's time to free your brain from parenting- and housekeeping-related thoughts and to give yourself a break from physical chores. It will take practice, and will likely feel uncomfortable at the beginning, but we all need to start somewhere.

EXERCISE 2: Investigate a method of play that you can enjoy

Think back to what you used to enjoy playing with as a child. What was your favourite toy or pastime? Did you have a hobby that has lapsed since you had children? Again, schedule in some time for 'playtime' each week. It doesn't have to be for long – fifteen minutes will do. Find something that isn't productive – something that has no ulterior motive aside from simply being fun.

EXERCISE 3: Introduce your children to the value of boredom

Try to have at least one day per week where you have nothing scheduled (aside from work and school, that is). Instead, just go with the flow and do whatever takes your fancy on the day, especially if that involves doing very little and relaxing. Help your children to learn that it's OK to do nothing by observing you doing the same. Just as you may have learned to be busy from your own parents, feeling discomfort with unplanned time, your children will learn to be comfortable with boredom – or not – from you.

EXERCISE 4: Practise different ways of saying 'no'

Try to come up with some of your own phrases to use with people when you uphold your own boundaries and say 'no'. Jot them down somewhere, so you can resort to them when necessary (especially for times when you feel uncomfortable declining). Once you have your stock phrases at the ready, see how often you can use them and notice how it gets a little easier each time you say 'no'.

EXERCISE 5: Notice your responses to the idea of doing less

When I suggest doing less to help with becoming a calmer parent, many instantly respond, 'But if I slow down, I get stressed, or I find I can't handle doing nothing, and my children are harder work.' If you can see yourself in this description, consider whether your busyness is truly serving you and helping you to be a calmer parent, or is it akin to the flight stress response (see page 23)? Is your busyness a learned behaviour that allows you to avoid any deeper feelings that may come with being still, or indeed coping with your child's behaviour when you do less? Is it possible that your busyness is actually making you more stressed, even though on the surface you believe it is helping?

In brief

I hope that this chapter has helped you to realise that busyness can often be a huge obstacle in the path to calmer parenting. Before we move on to the next chapter, here is a brief recap of some of the main points we have discussed here:

- Our culture views busyness as not only socially acceptable, but laudable. This view can cause us great harm.
- When we are busy and stretched to our limits, we are at risk of burnout, frayed tempers and increased stress and are more likely to engage in parenting that is anything but calm.
- We tend to try to solve problems by 'doing more', yet very often the answer is to 'do less'. Being aware of this unconscious bias is important if we are to become more comfortable with relaxation and down time.

- Don't be afraid to allow your children to become bored; boredom can be a blessing, whereas overscheduling your lives in the quest for entertainment can be exhausting and may also be counterproductive if your children never learn how to be OK with doing nothing.
- We must learn how to say 'no' and be comfortable with it. It is not wrong to have boundaries; in fact, they help us to be calmer because they allow us to concentrate on our own needs and not those of others.

We will pick up on the issue of boundaries again in the next chapter, when we speak about our relationships with others. Let's move on to these, and how they can impact our parenting, now.

Chapter 7

Relationships with Partners, Other Parents and Wider Family – and Why These Impact Your Relationship with Your Child

*Great relationships aren't great because they have
no problems. They're great because both people care
enough about the other to make it work!*

author unknown

There is no denying that the relationships we have with others have a huge impact on our state of mind and our parenting. When we feel well supported, everything is easier. Spending an hour or two in the company of a compassionate friend or family member can turn your day around, lifting your spirits and lightening your load. Sharing your worries and thoughts with your partner can make parenting much easier. As the saying goes: 'a problem shared is a problem halved'. Just a long chat with a distant friend, or sometimes even a like-minded stranger over the internet, can improve your mood and thus your relationship with your children. We are hard-wired for connection. We are a social species, meant to raise our young with the support of others. When this support is present and appropriate, we can thrive as parents and as individuals. When it is not, as is the case for so many parents today, we inevitably struggle and our calm crumbles.

When our relationships with other adults are fraught and strained, we tend to re-enact the difficult interactions with our children. Sometimes these difficult relationships are with our partners or ex-partners. Sometimes they are with our own parents, other family members or friends, and sometimes they are the result of stressful interactions with strangers or acquaintances via the internet. It doesn't matter what the source is – negative interactions with others all have the same impact on us: they threaten our calm and, consequently, our relationships and interactions with our children.

It isn't only difficult relationships that are problematic, though. Sometimes the sheer absence of close, supportive adult relationships can cause us to feel depleted, resentful, lonely and sad. Once again, these difficult emotions usually tumble out in our relationships with our children. We simply aren't meant to raise children alone, or alongside conflict with others, though the sad reality is that many of us are trying to do just that.

The importance of a tribe

We are meant to raise our children surrounded by the love, knowledge and physical and emotional input of others, both our contemporaries and those older and wiser than us. When I write about parenting as part of a tribe, I am always drawn to the parenting style of elephants. Elephants are known for raising their babies in a herd. If the elephant mama cannot do something for her baby, the aunts, older sisters and grandmothers all step in, often supplementing nursing, too. If an elephant baby is in danger, the whole herd will usually come to help. The herds are headed by a matriarch – an older, wiser female who leads with confidence, overseeing the close and loving connections of the younger members of the herd, each of whom plays their part, fulfilling their roles in support of others, while receiving unconditional support back. Emulating the social network of elephants sounds pretty good to me, but alas, we live in a culture that is disconnected, patriarchal and focused on the individual rather than the group.

Research has found that a social-support network helps parents to maintain a closer, more nurturing relationship with their children, with the need for this unsurprisingly being higher among mothers than fathers.[1] Speaking about the study findings, Associate Professor of Psychology Terese Glatz commented:

> A social-support network proved to be a help to mothers in their parenting role. The support may involve help of a practical nature, such as babysitting, as well as emotional support in the sense of having somebody who listens to you when you are having a hard time. For mothers who feel they are not in control of their lives, social support can help them build a better relationship with their children.

Naturally, this doesn't mean that fathers don't need support. Of course they do. It just means we should be especially aware of the importance of support networks for mothers, particularly new ones.

Further studies have considered the substantial impact that familial support provides for our emotional and physical wellbeing, not just during the early years of parenting, but throughout our whole lifespan.[2] What should you do if you don't have a tribe, though? Sadly, I think the lack of a tribe, or metaphorical village, is the norm, rather than the exception in our society today. The Covid-19 pandemic showed us all how important human connection is and hopefully helped us to value physical and emotional contact with others in a way that perhaps we didn't before. We live in a culture that is disconnected, though. Ironically, the more our world connects digitally, the further apart we all feel from each other. We must use the lessons that Covid taught us about the need for human connection and help to build back the community that we are all so sorely missing.

Acknowledging our need to connect is always the first step. The second must be actively doing something to meet it. Simply, I don't think we can wait for a tribe to appear around us. We are likely to be waiting all our lives if we do. If we don't have a tribe, and if we want one, we have no alternative – we must create one ourselves. This will often push us way outside of our comfort zones at a time when we are already desperately uncomfortable. But we must make new connections and build our own village. Nobody else is going to do it for us.

What parents say

I asked some parents about their adult friendships, the support they received from others and how this impacted on the relationship with their own children. Here's what they told me:

> I struggle when I see other families with lots of family help near by. My parents are four hours away and my in-laws six hours away. When I see grandparents collecting children from school it's a real trigger, as it makes me realise we are doing it alone with no one near by to rely on.

> I'm quite extroverted and I like seeing friends to re-energise. I can have a day at home with the kids, but if I have a couple of days (or more) where I only get to see my husband fleetingly in the evening and I only have a toddler and a baby to chat

with, then my mood gets quite low, and I find it hard to look after anyone else's tantrums.

We don't have the village that every parent needs, which makes it harder.

It's hard when you are raising kids just in a nuclear family with no support. Time together can easily become a burden instead of being cherished.

How do you make friends as an adult?

Do you remember being four years old and how easy it was to make friends with total strangers then? You could walk up to another child in the park, on the beach or in the school playground, talk about your favourite dinosaur, debating the attributes of a diplodocus versus a brontosaurus, or discuss your favourite Disney princess, or Marvel superhero, and within twenty minutes, you had found a new best friend. There was none of the anxiety, procrastinating and self-consciousness that accompanies the tricky world of adult friendships. Wouldn't it be wonderful if it were as easy to make friends now as it was back then? The thing is, there is nothing inherently different about friendships in adulthood; we just attach our adult worries to the process. We could learn a lot from watching blossoming friendships in childhood.

I've often thought it would be a great idea if there were special internet sites set up for adult friendship matchmaking – a little like dating websites (but hopefully a little less shallow). In the absence of this sort of service, we're left with the good old-fashioned techniques of friendship finding. However, I think we could utilise some of the processes used by dating services. These include:

- thinking about the type of person you would most like to be friends with; their rough age range, age of their children and location
- making a list of any hobbies and interests that you would like to share with a new friend
- noting the social activities that you would like to engage in with a new friend; for instance, are you looking for daytime coffee meets or evening parties?

Next, think about where you are most likely to find these people. Could they belong to a local club, gym or adult-education class? Are there parents you already chat with at the school gate who seem to have similar interests to you? What about internet chat groups? Or social media?

Once you've found a potential new friend, the next step is being brave and asking them out – not on a romantic date, but a meet-up at the park, a coffee after the school run, a quick drink after work or for a weekend walk. I think this is the hardest part because we're all equally anxious and worried about being rebuffed. The thing is, though, if you don't make the first move, and instead wait impatiently for others to offer the hand of friendship to you first, you could be waiting a lifetime. Maybe you've already met somebody you think you would like to be friends with and maybe they're just as nervous as you, waiting for you to say something first. What's the worst that would happen if they turned you down? Is the potential short-term embarrassment and dent to your confidence worth more than a future friendship that may revolutionise your life and your relationship with your child as a result?

What if your tribe makes you feel worse?

Of course, I've made a big assumption in this chapter so far that friendships and social tribes are always positive. But sometimes we find ourselves in groups that can leave us feeling lonelier than if we had no friends at all. Some friendships can be incredibly draining, some leave us questioning ourselves and our parenting choices and decisions far more than we'd like and some leave us feeling as if we do all the giving and get little in return. It's OK to let them go if they don't make you feel your best. Starting afresh is better than having a tribe that makes you feel worse when you're with them. If you feel uncomfortable in your current friendships, consider the following questions:

- Are you the one doing all the giving and the compromising?
- Does this friendship serve you still?
- Do they make you question your parenting, or your decisions?
- Do you still have lots in common?
- Do you feel better for spending time with this person?

If you answer 'no' to any of the above, maybe it's time to move on from the friendship? Maybe you were once great friends and you're holding on to the friendship because of the past. But people change, and it's OK to move on. Sometimes we make friends for life, sometimes we make friends for a season. If you can identify with the latter, maybe it's time to acknowledge the friendship for the joy that it brought to you but realise that now it is time to leave it behind, hopefully to find a better match for the current season, if not for life.

What if people don't like you (and the curse of people pleasing)?

I spent most of my teenage years and early twenties worrying that people didn't like me. As a result of my neuroses, I became a terrible people pleaser in my thirties. I would be the first to offer to do something if somebody asked for help, whether in real life or in an internet chat group. Somehow, I linked my self-worth with how people felt about me, and I believed that the best way to make people like me was to make them happy. Now, in my forties, I know that no matter what you say or do, there will be people who don't like you and that's OK. Some people are not going to like you based simply on what *they think* they know about you, and that's OK. We don't need to correct everybody's assumptions about us, and we don't need everybody to like us, no matter how much we think we do.

Are you guilty of always trying to help people, saying 'yes' to everything and volunteering to do things, no matter how thinly stretched you are? People pleasing has a terrible habit of pleasing everybody but yourself and is a huge source of overwhelm and burnout for so many parents. Often, it starts as parent pleasing in our childhoods; or rather, we people please because we only received love and attention from our parents when we did something 'good', meaning that our self-worth is now inextricably linked with the concept that we must earn affection from others. Sometimes we were raised with lots of praise and we now need to feel externally validated for what we do, so we people please as our primary stress response is to 'fawn' (see page 23) as a way to deal with discomfort and difficult situations.

Recognising that you tend to people please and understanding the underlying reasons is ultimately the best way to move away from it. It isn't selfish to say 'no', especially when you are otherwise struggling, and saying 'yes' all the time, jumping to the aid of others, doesn't make people think better of you. A friend who is only a friend because you are always doing things for them isn't really a friend at all. Conversely, a real friend will understand when you have to say 'no'. I'm not saying that you should never help others, just that a true friendship shouldn't be based on what you give and do. Helping others can help you to feel happier, not only because you release feelgood hormones when you help others, but because altruism can also help you to feel gratitude for what you have. There is a big difference, though, between helping others when you are able to and people pleasing, sacrificing your own needs to do so.

What if you're happier alone?

So far in this chapter I have focused on the importance of friendships with others and building a tribe around you to support you in your parenting. Some people, however, are genuinely happier alone. If this is the case for you, please don't think that I'm implying there is something wrong with you. What I'm really trying to say, is that for those who need a tribe, the lack of one can be incredibly damaging, but for others, who thrive on their own, or with only one close friend, the solitude can be affirming. If you are happier alone, then embracing your need for solitude, rather than questioning if there is something wrong with you, is the way to go. Introversion is not a flaw, neither is the need to spend time alone – the key is in knowing what is right for you and embracing it.

What does a positive relationship look like?

Many adults move from one difficult relationship to another. Often, this cycle is rooted in our own upbringings, as discussed in Chapter 1. If we didn't have a positive relationship with our own parents as children, then, without this role model, we can find ourselves in relationships and friendships that don't serve us as adults. So what should a positive relationship – whether this is a parent–child, romantic or platonic relationship – look like?

- Both parties should feel equally supported.
- Both parties should feel equally heard and valued.
- Both parties should be honest with each other, with open communication.
- Both parties should trust each other.
- There should be an equal balance of power, whereby neither party exerts more control than the other.
- Both parties should respect the independence of the other, allowing and encouraging them to have positive relationships with others.
- Decisions should be made collaboratively, taking into consideration the feelings of both parties equally, and without fear of retaliation or retribution.
- Both parties should have shared activities, but should still retain individual identities.
- Both parties should have boundaries that are mutually respected.

In addition, the following have no place in a positive relationship:

- **Co-dependency**: this is different to dependency, which happens when two people rely on each other for mutual support and the relationship is beneficial to both parties. Co-dependency works on an imbalance of support, where one party is always sacrificing for the other and only feels good when they are needed and the other party, known as the enabler, feels good for having their needs always met by the other.
- **An imbalance of control**: where one party controls all decisions made or the other party is scared of making decisions, for fear of retribution. This could be anything from control of finances, to control of social activities.
- **Physical or mental abuse**: this could range from hitting to constantly calling the other party names, belittling, controlling or gaslighting them; the abuser tries to make the other party feel as if everything is their fault and that they are the problem when, in fact, the problem is the abuser. This is often accompanied by dishonesty and disrespect.

If anything in this section rings alarm bells for you, you can find some contacts, further reading and support organisations who can help in the Resources section on page 233. You will also find some information on how to improve your adult relationships at the end of this chapter.

What parents say

I spoke with some parents about their relationships and how they often triggered difficult feelings and behaviours. Here's what they told me:

> I find my calm completely goes out the window when I'm frustrated with my partner about something. My

four-year-old's behaviour can then trigger a reaction from me that isn't calm or fair, and often totally disproportionate, and I end up taking out all my frustrations on her in that moment. I feel so guilty as I know this is what I'm doing but struggle with this the most.

... when I'm exhausted from being up with the baby all night and in the day my husband repeatedly yawns, then says he needs a nap, even though he's had a full night's sleep, and he chose to stay up late watching TV. No care for how tired I am. Watching him yawn is really triggering for me.

I really struggle when others comment on my children's or my own behaviour, particularly my mum, when she says something like: 'Yes, I know you're doing it like that but ...'

I really struggle when my other half undoes all the gentle parenting I've done in the day by saying something like, 'If you don't tidy up, I'll take all the toys away,' regardless of the number of times we've spoken about why we aren't using those phrases any more and the effect they have.

I find it hard to stay calm when my other half is not being as supporting as I feel she could be, or almost coming across as contradictory to me in situations. Like when she makes a plan and enacts it without checking what might already be planned or what I might like to do.

Relatives watching or commenting on my parenting stresses me out and I struggle not to transfer this to the kids. I find this worst with my own mum as she's outwardly critical yet was ... is a horrible mother.

When your relatives and friends make you feel bad about your parenting

A common theme that runs through questions I am often asked by parents who are struggling with their relationships centres on unsolicited or unwelcome parenting advice. Often given by older generations, this advice can really undermine your instincts and beliefs and cause you to second-guess yourself. This anxiety can then result in dissatisfaction with parenting and have a knock-on effect on your ability to stay calm with your children. So how can you respond to the unwanted advice that is so often given?

Try to see the motivation

A lot of what we view as criticism can really be classified as well-meant concern. This is particularly true if it comes from those close to us, such as relatives. Perhaps they are worried about how tired you look, or they are genuinely concerned about your child, and rather than meaning to attack what you are doing, their comments are aimed at (what they believe will be) something far healthier for your child and you. The comments may come out wrong and it can be easy to perceive them as being an attack on you, but I think most criticism is just poorly phrased concern. Of course, this isn't always the case, and sometimes people are just negative, interfering busybodies, but I find trying to look for the motivation really helpful.

Understand they are speaking from their own knowledge and experience base

When my firstborn was a baby, early weaning, cry-based sleep training and punishments as the main approach to discipline were the in thing. These were advised in all the baby books, by health visitors and child nurses, official healthcare publications and television experts. Things have changed a lot in the past two decades, so imagine how much they have changed over the past thirty or forty decades! I have kept up to date with current research and recommendations because that's my job; if it wasn't, I'd have no reason to know how much things have changed and I would likely believe that the same recommendations still applied. People give advice and criticise based upon what they know and believe to be true. Similarly, they criticise and advise based upon their own experiences, both of being a child and (sometimes) raising one. This involves a lot of cognitive dissonance (where you subconsciously convince yourself that something isn't true, as a form of self-protection) because accommodating new, updated advice means admitting that how they were raised, or how they raised their own children, may have been damaging. And instead of admitting this and working through the big feelings it brings, many people will attack the new information – sometimes consciously, other times totally subconsciously. In a sense, the fact you are doing things differently may be seen as an attack on what they did or are doing. Hence, their criticism of you is a defence mechanism. Basically, their negative words are not saying anything about you, but everything about them.

Ask questions and talk about emotions

If you want to respond to the advice or criticism, my strongest suggestion is to hold back on piling the evidence on the person who is giving it. I see so many posts on social media saying things like, 'Can anyone provide me with some research showing sleep training is bad?' Providing evidence here is totally ineffective. Why? Because it just won't get through the cognitive-dissonance barrier. The person in question probably won't even read it. And if they do read it, they will dismiss it.

So what works better than hard evidence? Two things: asking 'why?' and appealing to their emotions. The next time somebody says, 'He needs to sleep in his own room,' ask them why. Keep drilling down and drilling down. When they say, 'Because he needs to be independent,' ask why. When they say, 'Because he won't ever learn to be alone otherwise,' ask why. At some point, they will reach a dead end and simply not be able to answer. Or there is a slim chance they may realise that their criticism has no substance and what they read/saw is incorrect (though don't hold your breath!). The other tactic is to appeal to their emotions. Here, I like to ask them to put themselves into the child's place or imagine how they felt, or what they needed as a child. 'How do you think she feels when she's left crying in her cot?' or, 'Do you remember a time when you really needed your parents, but they didn't come for you?' In my experience, asking 'why?' and appealing to emotions is infinitely more successful than providing evidence.

Smile and thank them

Also known as 'simply ignore them'! But this needs to be done in a way that makes them feel they've been listened to. Rather than saying, 'Please keep your opinions to yourself!' or, 'No, I'm not doing that,' responses like, 'Thanks for your advice. I'll take it on board,' or, 'OK, that's definitely something to think about,' quieten people a lot quicker. Sure, you have not done anything to attempt to change their minds, but I think sometimes, for our own sanity, it's best to smile nod, ignore and move on. We're not here to change the world for everybody, just for our children. It's OK if somebody holds a conflicting view to yours.

Remind yourself of why you're doing things this way

These last two points are about keeping your confidence up because criticism and unwanted advice can really erode it. If you've been on the receiving end from several people, or over a sustained length of time, it can be all too easy to start questioning yourself. Take a breather to remind yourself of why you're doing this your way – reread the books and the articles, watch a video, listen to a podcast. Revisit whatever source convinced you in the first place. If that source was your intuition, or heart, then try to switch off from all things parenting and go for a long walk, watch a movie, read a (non-parenting) book, meditate and do whatever it is that you enjoy doing to take away some of the toxicity.

Get support from like-minded parents

It can be hard parenting in a way that is not the norm. Time surrounded by people doing things differently to you is hard going, especially if they criticise you. The best solution I've found for this is to surround yourself with like-minded people. People who agree with you. Post on the internet about your experience in a group that matches your parenting style (see Resources, page 233, for recommendations); the replies that agree with you and tell you to ignore the criticisms can be incredibly validating. Which brings us back to the idea of creating a tribe around you.

Should you end toxic relationships?

If your relationship with a certain family member or friend is proving to be incredibly stressful, putting a stop to the toxicity by ending the relationship is sometimes the only way to go, for the sake of yourself and your children, your sense of calm and your parenting. However, if it is not possible to end the relationship (here, I'm not talking about romantic relationships, but more those with toxic or narcissistic parents that for whatever reason cannot be broken), you may find a technique known as 'stonewalling' helpful. This aims to end the criticism and toxicity in their tracks the moment they start. Simply, you make it clear that an issue is not open to debate or discussion, by giving very brief answers – just 'yes' or 'no', for example – or changing the subject immediately.

Note: you should understand that stonewalling is incredibly damaging to relationships and is often discussed as a form of abuse, or control. It is not the solution to problems in romantic relationships; rather, it will only add to difficulties in these situations. The conscious intention to stonewall is used as a protection mechanism for you in an already toxic relationship that is unavoidable and unsalvageable and where all other techniques and approaches to improve things have failed.

What if you and your partner (or ex-partner) disagree on parenting styles?

Ideally, parenting style is something that all adults will talk to their partners about before they have children. As well as researching birth plans and nursery products, I truly believe that discussing parenting opinions is vital before the first baby arrives. Too many couples realise that they have opposing views on parenting several months or years down the line. So as well as writing a birth plan, parents-to-be should also write a parenting plan, thinking about common scenarios and how they might respond to them. I particularly love it when a pregnant couple attend one of my gentle discipline talks or workshops.

But what do you do if the differences in your parenting beliefs surface further down the line? Research has shown that differences in parenting opinions can place a huge strain on a relationship that is already under increased strain due to the transition to parenting.[3]

First, you have to acknowledge your partner's feelings and try to understand where they come from. Often, if somebody has been raised in a certain way (and says, 'It never did me any harm'), for the other partner to say that they would like to do things differently is a bit of an insult to their in-laws. Acknowledging this is an important first step. Next, ask your partner (without judgement) why they feel the way they do and how they would deal with certain scenarios. Also, ask if they know of any research to back up their thoughts.

Once you have thoroughly listened to your partner, explain to them how you feel, why you feel the way you do and offer a brief synopsis of any supporting research (though do remember, as previously mentioned, this is usually the least effective method of trying to convince someone of parenting in a different way). Consider media they may like. Do they read blogs, magazine articles or books, or do they prefer videos or podcasts? Perhaps they would do better with in-person learning, such as workshops. Be careful of the wording you use here. Don't use accusatory language like, 'You're really rough when you shout,' or, 'When you did that it really scared her.' Instead, use 'I' statements and clarify your emotions: 'I feel uncomfortable when you shout at her,' for example.

The next step is to try to agree on tiny baby steps, rather than everything at once. Perhaps your partner will agree to change their language slightly and drop the word 'naughty' or similar for a week or two. That's enough to start with. Don't try for too much too soon. The next decision could be to try to stop threatening punishments and instead use empathising language. The beauty of gentle discipline is that the results are fairly obvious. They may be slow (sometimes frustratingly so), but there will be a 'breakthrough' moment that makes your partner think, Wow, that worked.

Deal with one issue at a time and maintain open (and non-accusatory/non-judgemental) discussion throughout. It can also be really helpful to meet up with others disciplining the same way as you, particularly those of the same gender as your partner. Role modelling is very powerful and many of us lack this when it comes to parenting.

What if you have no family support?

So far, this chapter has focused on difficult relationships with our families, but what if you have no family support? This is something very close to home for me. As mentioned earlier, I am an only child, my mother died when I was twenty-one and my father died three years later, exactly nine months before my first child was born. My husband's parents both died shortly after my children were born and so we found ourselves entirely alone. Newly orphaned new parents. Obviously, I have no idea how it feels to raise children with difficult and toxic relationships with your own parents or siblings, but I do know how it feels to be totally alone, unsupported and thoroughly lost. There have been countless times when I have felt deeply jealous when I've seen a new mum out with her baby and her mother, or a grandfather picking up a grandchild from school. My children have never known what it is like to be loved by anyone other than their father and me, and I have never known what it is like to be a parent, while also being a child and being parented myself.

It is easy to slip into bitterness in this situation. A hole I found myself in all too often in the early years of parenting. Now I'm aware that sinking into this hole, the deep darkness of 'if only' and 'why me?' serves nobody. It makes me angry, it makes me sad and it makes me anything but a calm parent. The one slight positive I take away from not having parents when I became one myself is wondering if it was easier never knowing what it feels like to have my parents disapprove of my parenting choices. I will never know if they are proud of me as a parent, but I will never feel let down by them either. I like to take some comfort in the fact that our relationships ended on a high.

Twenty years into motherless (and fatherless) mothering, I have learned the only way to go is with acceptance, gratitude for the past and looking forwards to the future with the hope that I will be able to support my own children in a way that I never was myself. I am also retrospectively aware that in the early years I probably would have benefited hugely from some professional support and counselling, which is why I have included some information about support organisations and further reading in the Resources on page 233.

Tips to improve your relationships

I want to end this chapter with some actionable tips to help you improve the relationships you have with others in your life. This, in turn, can help you to be a calmer parent for your children.

Communicate, communicate, communicate

The golden rule of good relationships is surely communication. We must learn how to communicate better with each other, which involves listening just as much as talking. Many relationship problems start when we assume that others understand our feelings and motives. We also wind ourselves up when we presume that we know how others think and feel, imagining their thought processes in our mind. These assumptions are often incorrect and, as the saying goes, 'When we assume, we make an ASS out of U and ME.' Instead, the answer is listening and talking to each other – not listening so that we can talk or answer back, but rather listening so that we can understand. Relationship issues are not usually just one person's problem, but both, and if we are to understand the other person's thoughts and feelings we need to get better at communicating. What can you take from this into your own life?

Learn how to disagree

Good relationships happen when we have things in common with other people, and when we respect each other for our differences. It's OK that we hold different points of view. It's OK to have different beliefs. It's *not* OK to disrespect each other because of our differences. Sometimes relationship difficulties happen when we are intent on changing somebody's mind or making them think more like us, but respecting difference is often the best way to keep a relationship – and the other partner – happy and also to have our own opinions respected, too. Is there something your friend, relative or partner believes that you disagree with, but could learn to be more respectful of?

You don't have to join every fight you're invited to

When was the last time you got drawn into an argument between your parent and sibling, or two friends, or even two strangers on the internet? It's very easy to spring to the defence of one party or jump in and join the argument, but we should remember that not every disagreement is meant for us. We don't have to join every fight we're invited to. Sometimes it is a lot better to protect our peace of mind and stay neutral. Can you try to apply this the next time you feel yourself getting drawn into an argument that doesn't have anything to do with you? Maybe it's time to hit the 'block' button on social media (something I have done a lot recently and enjoy a much greater sense of calm for doing so).

Embrace the wiggly lines

Just like almost every aspect of life, relationships don't move in a nice, straight line. Even the best friendships or family or romantic relationships have their ups and downs. There will be times when you get on famously and times when everything feels much heavier. This is normal and it's OK. It doesn't mean there is anything wrong with your relationship, or with you, or the other party. Life naturally ebbs and flows, just as relationships move in a wiggly line. Don't focus too much on the down days; instead, have faith that they will soon be on the up again if you ride out the dip. Where are you in the wiggly line of your relationship at the moment? Can you see the possibility of an uplift in the future?

Schedule time to talk (and listen)

When we're busy with work, raising children and the demands of everyday life, it can be incredibly difficult to sit down and have a deep and honest conversation with someone. All too often, issues are brushed aside or buried because it seems impossible to find time to discuss them. The trouble is, they don't disappear. They stay there, often growing, unnoticed, until they are so big that they seem almost insurmountable. By keeping on top of our worries and concerns and scheduling regular time to discuss any problems, we can keep our relationships as healthy as possible. Can you plan some time with your partner, co-parent, friend or family member to calmly discuss anything that is bothering you before it becomes a much bigger problem?

Write a letter

Sometimes we can find it hard to put our true feelings and emotions into words. We try and everything comes out wrong, or we struggle to find the words and end up brushing our concerns aside because it feels like the wrong time, or the wrong way to raise them. These unaired feelings then fester until they explode at a later date, not necessarily because of anything the other person has done but because we have sat on them for so long. Or, worse still, we explode at our children, triggered by something entirely unrelated and out of proportion. If you struggle to voice your worries, writing a letter can help you to make more sense of your feelings and present them in a calmer, controlled way that is more likely to be received well by the other party. They, in turn, can then read the letter at a time that is best for them and spend some time thinking about their response, rather than doing or saying something in the heat of the moment. Perhaps after writing the letter you may even decide not to send it, and destroy it instead, but the very act of getting everything out and down onto paper is freeing in itself. Either way, letter writing may seem old-fashioned in the age of texts and instant messages, but it can be a really helpful tool for positive relationships. Is there anything you feel would be better written down in a letter?

In brief

Before we move on to the next chapter, I thought it would be a good idea to round up some of the most important points we have covered about relationships in this chapter:

- The relationships we have with others have a huge impact on how we feel and how we act towards our own children.
- We are not meant to raise children alone. Like other mammals, we need a tribe, or a herd, to help and to hold us, especially when the road is tough.
- It is often harder to make friends as an adult but remembering the friendships of our childhoods can help us. Often, others are as desperate for us to make the first move as we are for them to do so. Being brave and taking the first step is important.
- Friendships change and sometimes we find we have friends for a season, rather than friends for life. Recognising the difference and acknowledging when a friendship no longer serves us helps to keep our relationships positive.
- People pleasing, with its roots often firmly in our past,

serves nobody, least of all ourselves. Remember, it's OK for people to not like you, and if they only like you because of what you do for them, then they aren't your people.

- Communication and empathy are the key to all relationships. Understanding the other person's point of view, whether that's your own parent, your partner or ex-partner, is the best way forward.
- Sometimes, if a relationship is particularly toxic, it is in everybody's interests, especially your children's, to end the relationship if you can.
- All relationships need work and have ups and downs. This is normal and not a sign that the relationship is unsalvageable, but rather, a wake-up call to communicate better.

I hope that this chapter has helped you to understand the relationships in your life a little more, and how they can impact on those you have with your children and your ability to stay calm. It is a sad reality that very often, the roots of our own anger and dysregulation have nothing to do with what our children have said or done, but everything to do with how supported – or otherwise – we are feeling. However, good relationships are necessary not just for becoming better parents for our children; they are also essential for our own emotional wellbeing and happiness, something we all very much deserve.

Chapter 8

Balancing Work and Home Life – Why We Must Stop Aiming to 'Have It All'

I've learned that making a living is not the same thing as making a life.

Maya Angelou, poet

I once read the following on the internet and it has stuck with me ever since: 'Parents are expected to work like they don't have children and parent as if they don't work.' That short sentence (author unknown) sums up everything I feel about working and raising a family today. Working parents feel torn in two, with expectations placed upon them in the work-place to work just as hard, if not harder, than their childless colleagues and by society to be perfect parents, regardless of work pressures and commitments. We simply can't win. If we don't work and focus on full-time parenting, we are labelled as lazy, especially if we claim welfare benefits to tide us over for a year or two. If we do work, we're thought to be neglectful, supposedly placing our careers above our children's needs. I have often wondered what balance of work versus stay-at-home parenting would be considered ideal? I've never found out – because it doesn't exist.

So whether you work or not, it's a case of damned if you do, damned if you don't. Our society is sadly unsupportive of all parents, but particularly those who try to juggle the demands of family life with those of their professional lives. What happens when this lack of support, understanding and perceptions of judgement coincide? The guilt runs deep inside us, coursing through every vein. We feel guilty when we focus on our work, worrying about the impact our dedication has upon our children and we feel guilty when we focus on our children, worrying about the impact our dedication has upon our careers. What is the result of all this worry and guilt? Usually, our mental health is the casualty, in our quest to not let anybody down, we tend to put ourselves and our own needs last and that in turn creates the physical and emotional burnout that we know all too well eats away at our ability to be a calm parent.

What is the answer? I honestly don't know. It's something I've grappled with for the last two decades, ever since I gave up a high-flying career in the pharmaceutical industry to be a full-time mother. The disbelief and shock I was met with when I announced that I had decided to be '*just* a stay-at-home mother' for a few years was telling. People thought I was crazy. Why would I give up such a promising career to raise a child? What a waste! Fast-forward a few years and my dreams of Walton-esque full-time parenting – milling around the house and garden with my impeccably behaved children, followed by wafts of PlayDoh, daisy chains and home-baked bread – didn't pan out and I found myself desperate to work again. The guilt I felt when I finally admitted to myself that although I loved them dearly, staying home with my children was not enough for me was immense. I needed to work – not just to pay the bills, but for my sanity, too. I craved adult conversation and I desperately wanted to use my brain again. I also wanted to work to set an example to my children, especially my daughter. And so I returned to the world of work and realised that whatever I did, I would be judged, I would feel guilty, I would struggle mentally and physically and I would always wonder if I had made the right decision. In some ways I think accepting this was the most important thing I did. No decision would end with me feeling completely at peace; no decision would be easy.

The guilt of being a working parent

The guilt that accompanies being a working parent is especially painful. There are so many 'firsts' to make you feel bad.

- The first time you drop your child at day care and have to leave them sobbing, holding their arms out to you, desperate for you to stay
- The first time they walk, or speak, and you miss it because you're at work
- The first time they hurt themselves while you're at work, and you can't be there to comfort them
- The first time you miss a school assembly or sports day
- The first time you have to leave them when they are sick
- The first time you have to leave them at a day camp in the school holidays, while your friends are enjoying special family days out
- The first time your child is desperate to talk to you about their day, but you have an urgent email to respond to, or meeting to attend, and you have to tell them that you can't listen to them yet
- The first time you get home late from work and your child is already asleep in bed and you realise you have barely seen them for nearly twenty-four hours
- The first time you go away on a work trip and don't get to kiss them goodnight.

And this doesn't even include the guilt that you experience around work. The guilt when you're so tired from a sleepless night that you make a silly mistake. The guilt when you're so exhausted you can't concentrate in a meeting. The guilt when your colleague has to shoulder more than their fair share because you just can't put in more hours than you're doing already. And the guilt when it takes you much longer than it should to reply to an email or contact an important client.

We constantly feel pulled in all directions, sometimes so much so that it feels as if we are being torn in two. Working parents simply cannot avoid the guilt.

In a recent YouGov poll of 4500 adults, over a third of respondents revealed that they believed they spent too much time at work and not enough with their children.[1] This figure was highest among parents of children under one. We struggle more with guilt about parenting and working than we do at any other time.

Working-parent guilt is, perhaps unsurprisingly, felt more keenly by mothers. We live in a society that still holds sexist beliefs, with a largely unspoken rule that mothers should be primarily responsible for raising the children. The YouGov poll mentioned above found that just under a third of respondents believed this, while almost 40 per cent believed that fathers should be primarily responsible for working and bringing in money for the family. Research has found that heterosexual families often see an unequal division of parenting duties, even when both partners work,[2] with mothers being more than twice as likely as fathers to handle the majority of caregiving responsibilities and significantly more likely to have to take time off work to care for sick children. The sad reality is that mothers not only bear the brunt of childcare, regardless of whether they work or not, but they tend to feel working-parent guilt more keenly, too.

Coping with the guilt

So what do you do with the oppressive guilt that so often accompanies working as a parent? Especially when that guilt can spill out as stress, frustration and anger directed towards your children, the following tips can help:

- Acknowledge that what you are doing is exceptionally hard. We simply aren't meant to raise a family and work full-time at the same time. In essence, being a working parent is like having two full-time jobs and a whole lot of extra overtime. There are only so many hours in the day and it just isn't possible to do everything. This isn't your fault. It's the fault of the society you live in. It feels hard because it is hard.
- Change your expectations for yourself. Most of our guilt comes from when we set unrealistically high goals for ourselves and fail to meet them, for example when we can't be the parent we envisioned, and we also can't meet the standards we set for ourselves in our careers. Accepting that we need to lower the bar a little, both at home and at work, allows us to feel better about both roles.
- Realise that you are not alone. Sometimes if may feel as if every other working parent is sailing through life, but they aren't. Maybe they're not being honest about how hard they're finding things, or maybe they just don't share their real feelings, but they absolutely feel the same as you. Also, be careful of comparison (as discussed in Chapter 3); it can be especially hard on working parents.
- Recognise the positives that being a working parent brings to your life and your family, whether that is the material things you can afford, the little extras, the gratitude you feel when you get to spend one-on-one time with your children

or the fact that some time away with other adults helps you to be a better parent when you are with your child.

- Understand that children are resilient and don't need you to be with them constantly, or to nail parenting when you are. Good enough really is good enough. This is something we will discuss again in Chapter 10.

Ultimately, I don't think any one thing can absolve of us the guilt that accompanies being a working parent, although I do believe the very fact that we feel guilty is a good sign. It indicates how deeply we care and that is possibly one of the best attributes a parent (and a worker) can have.

It isn't just the guilt, though

If only it were as simple as 'just' feeling guilt as a working parent. Life would be a lot simpler if we only had to worry about the thoughts running through our minds. Alas, working and parenting at the same time bring several other worries too:

- **The stress of getting everybody ready in the mornings, and out of the door on time.** There are no magic solutions here, I'm afraid, but planning and preparation are your friends. Prep and plan everything you can the night before, leaving as little as possible to do in the morning. Plus – however much you are desperate to hit that alarm 'snooze' button just one more time – getting up earlier is probably the ultimate solution to constantly running late. A stressed and hurried child is usually far less co-operative than a slightly tired one.
- **Worries about childcare.** Again, this draws on our support networks, or rather lack of them, as mentioned in the previous chapter. We're lucky if we have involved parents

and siblings who can take care of our children and help
with school runs, standing in for us during times of illness
and so on, but without this tribe around us, childcare
can be exceptionally hard. I wish I had something to
suggest here, but I don't. All I can offer is my sympathy
and empathy. Childcare in our society sucks. I don't mean
those that offer the care – they are usually underpaid
heroes. I mean the fact that government views childcare
as a second-class occupation, consistently underfunding it
while demanding more from the workers. What we need
is recognition for the ridiculously important role childcare
workers play in our lives, proper funding and more flexible
working arrangements, something we'll discuss a little later
in this chapter.

- **Coping with the lack of downtime.** Maybe one of the
  hardest things about parenting and working, especially
  full-time, is the inability to be able to switch off at the
  end of the day. You simply leave one job and go straight
  into another. When do you get a break? The sad answer
  is – you don't. You're always on duty and with the constant
  vigilance comes the very real risk of burnout. In the next
  chapter, we will discuss a few ways that you can take more
  care of yourself, in body and in mind, to hopefully lighten
  the burden just a little.

- **Having to get up and function professionally after a
  night of little or no sleep.** We have previously discussed
  how working parents find their role hardest during a child's
  first year – the months when sleep becomes a distant
  memory and parenting requires you to give your all, and
  then some, physically. Again the answer here really lays at
  the feet of government. We must improve parental leave and
  we must also make the workplace a more supportive and
  hospitable place for new parents. Sadly, I have worked with
  so many new parents who, absolutely desperate, believe that

the only solution is to sleep-train and prematurely wean
their babies. Yet the babies are the only party here that
don't have a problem – they are simply sleeping like babies.
They shouldn't have to be the ones to change, and neither
should we. We must demand more from those who run our
countries and our companies.

- **The relentlessness of self-employment.** So far in this
  chapter, I have focused on those who are employed by
  others. But what about those who are self-employed? (I
  count myself in this category.) We get no time off at all –
  because you can't shut down your laptop or turn off your
  email notifications when you're self-employed. What if you
  miss an important enquiry or client? There is no holiday
  pay. No (liveable) sick pay or (realistic) parental leave. We
  have to work through illness (I was answering client emails
  within twenty-four hours of major surgery last year), we
  have to work through our fourth trimesters (I taught a
  class less than a week after my fourth baby arrived) and
  we can never switch off. I tell you these things, not from
  some sort of twisted need for admiration, but because now
  I look back, I can't believe how ridiculously stupid I was in
  both instances. I love being self-employed, but sometimes I
  wonder if we have the worst of both worlds? What we gain
  in flexibility and the enjoyment of being our own bosses,
  we lose in the sheer inability to ever take time off and the
  worry that we must keep on keeping on at all times in
  order to keep business rolling in. The only advice I can give
  you here is that, once again, it's easy to hit burnout when
  you're self-employed, so although saying 'no' and having
  boundaries may feel exceptionally hard at first (turning a
  client down when you're not sure how you're going to make
  your next month's mortgage or rent payment is possibly
  one of the scariest things you will ever do), it's essential
  if you are going to keep functioning and thriving, both

professionally and personally. Self-imposed down time is essential, too, if you are to avoid risking burnout, which will, ultimately, cost you more than a lost client or two. I've learned the hard way that it's better to leave an email unanswered, than rush in and reply at any cost.

I'm quite sure that I haven't mentioned all the problems that accompany being a working parent here, but I hope I have helped you to realise quite what an awesome job you're doing in the face of such adversity. And one thing I *am* sure of is that you are doing an awesome job!

What parents say

When researching this chapter, I spoke with some working parents and asked them how they juggled work and home life, and how they felt it affected their parenting. Here's what they told me:

> I struggle with being tired and having a million things running through my mind about other stuff – usually work-related. When I am feeling stressed with work, I am far quicker to snap or get annoyed by normal behaviours from my children.

> Being the breadwinner, working full-time and trying to have a successful career, while also trying to be a good parent is hard, and causes high stress levels.

> … when I've had a stressful day at work. Then go home with a super-clingy child who just wants to reaffirm our connection by crawling into my skin, but I've not managed to unwind and desperately need to get the dinner and chores

done. And really all I want to do is not leave her in the first place, so the guilt adds to the stress.

I struggle when I've not had time to compartmentalise my work day before I have to parent.

I really struggle with the general motherhood expectations and paradoxes. Like you should have a job but do everything in the home. But if you have a job, you don't care about your child. But if you're a stay-at-home mother, then you're lazy, etc.

I really struggle with work stress. I'm a teacher, so when I've had a bad day at work, I've had to try really hard to be patient with the children I teach and when I get home, I just haven't got any left for my own children.

The day before work (particularly night-time) has me so stressed out; I know I'm rushing bedtime and bathtime, but it is so hard. I start planning for work and stressing by early evening.

The positives of being a working parent

I think it's about time that we added a little positivity to this chapter, don't you? Being a working parent is bloody tough, but it can also be pretty amazing, and I don't think we speak about the benefits enough. Here are just a few of them:

- **Working helps you to find yourself, outside of parenting.**
  I often speak to new parents, mothers in particular, who say,

'I feel like I don't know who I am any more,' or, 'I feel like I've lost the old me.' Of course, you are an entirely different person once you have children and will never go back to the old you because you have changed immeasurably. That change isn't bad – it has added so many more layers to the person you were pre-children – but it can erode your identity and leave your grappling for a sense of self and worth. Working outside of the home (or rather in a career outside of child-raising, if you work from home) can help to speed the transition of matrescence and patrescence (see page 102), enabling you to hold on to a sense of the former you while your metamorphosis takes place.

- **Working helps you to fulfil your purpose.** This is really a continuation of the previous point. Working allows you to find your sense of purpose and belonging in the world. Once we have children, our goals shift, often centring entirely on our children. For many, though, this is unfulfilling, and the lack of purpose, passion and drive in their lives can lead them to be irritated more at their children. Finding your purpose again takes the pressure off your children. Society may tell you that your purpose should be your children, and anything else is selfish, but that's just not true. You don't need to conform, and your life doesn't have to solely revolve around your children (unless you want it to, of course). Personally, I take a huge amount from my work with parents. I find it incredibly fulfilling and feel that it gives me as much as I give to them. It feels good to have a purpose that is distinct from my purpose as a mother.
- **You get time to think and decompress on the commute.** That blissful hour or two on the train, bike or in the car – listening to music, podcasts or audiobooks, or reading the daily paper – is blissful and so important for our souls. It's enforced self-care in a world that is constantly demanding

more and more from us. Try hard to embrace it and not make the commute a extension of your work day.

- **You get valuable time with other adults, to talk about things other than parenting.** Never, ever underestimate the impact of time spent with other adults talking about adult things, unrelated to parenting. After days focused on Peppa Pig, Bing, Minecraft or Fortnite, just half an hour spent speaking to another adult can be a balm to the soul – not least because it takes your mind off the pressures of parenting and the guilt of being a working parent, albeit temporarily.

- **You get much needed time away from your children.** Following on from the previous point, I will be the first to admit that I am a better parent if I get to spend regular time away from my children. I think a lot of people are shocked when they hear me say this because I always talk about attachment and the importance of connection. However, it is much easier to offer a secure attachment to our children when we fulfil our own needs and allow ourselves some space when we need it. Parenting can be, and is, stifling. Time apart from our children allows us to make the space necessary to contain them when we are with them and helps us to appreciate them much more.

I know that I am a better parent for working. That doesn't mean that I don't still get pangs of guilt now and again. I think that's unavoidable. However, I know for my family that we are all better off if I work, and I don't just mean materially and financially. I am a better mother for having my own passions and my own headspace. I would wager that the same is true for you, too (if you do work, that is).

What parents say

When chatting with parents about working and parenting, several told me that working, particularly outside of the home, really helped them to be calmer parents.

> This might sound counterintuitive but working helps me be a calmer parent! Having two or three days a week working outside the home, doing something I enjoy, means I appreciate the time with my children a lot more and I am a lot more patient as a result.

> Having a career really helps to keep me sane. I love my children, but I also love using my knowledge, interacting with other adults daily and keeping my brain ticking. I get a real sense of achievement and I feel it helps my self-esteem, which I think makes me a better parent.

> I love the work commute! I get two hours every day where I can unwind, read a book or the newspaper and listen to music. Those two hours daily are vital for helping me to be a calm parent.

Working from home – has it made things easier, or just different?

The world of work changed instantly in the spring of 2020 with the arrival of the Covid pandemic. Overnight, offices, nurseries and schools were closed, and many found themselves working from home. Obviously, this was not the case for all, with heroic keyworkers and others still commuting to their regular place of work, but it did bring about a huge change in the way we work for a lot of us. On the one hand, it offered more flexibility and a chance to spend more time with our children; on the other, it brought fresh challenges, including the following:

- Lack of a dedicated, quiet workspace, where parents were able to work undisturbed and in relative comfort
- Having to source the hardware and technology needed for working from home
- A lack of childcare, meaning that working parents had to balance full-time work and full-time parenting simultaneously
- Virtual schooling, meaning working parents had to balance full-time work and full-time teaching simultaneously (often balanced with caring for younger children, too)
- A lack of face-to-face contact with other adults.

While the pandemic brought about many unique and incredibly difficult challenges, it also taught us one very important thing about working – the fact that it is possible to do it flexibly. The pandemic showed many organisations that parents can be productive working from home. We must be better prepared for it, though, and more flexibility must be offered and encouraged, rather than having to fit our working lives into our current lives and homes, as we have been doing. As first steps go, though, it was a pretty important one, with hurdles that are not insurmountable. Is Covid a step towards a more flexible working life? I really hope so.

What are the answers – or rather, the questions?

Recent world events have put working parents centre stage, and we are finally starting to ask the questions that we should have asked – and demanded answers to – many, many years ago. So what are the questions we should be asking as working parents in order to make our lives a little easier? I believe the following are a good start:

- **Can we have more flexibility?** Flexibility at work doesn't just mean the option to work remotely (although that is important), it also means the opportunity to work flexible hours, to job share and to work part-time. It also means being able to work in different locations, not just at home or in an office located in a big city – options such as co-working spaces and hot desking are an example here.
- **Can we have better parental leave?** We need to work towards offering both parents their own individual quota of parental leave, rather than splitting it between the two. For instance, a father's time off shouldn't be at the expense of a mother's; and fathers, in particular, should be encouraged to take time off and reassured that it won't be to the detriment of their careers. (Research has shown fathers are still unlikely to take the paternity leave on offer to them.[3] In a survey of almost 2000, 53 per cent of fathers took no paternity leave at all.)
- **Can we have better support in the workplace for working parents?** Special policies for working parents should be introduced, covering elements such as time off for sick children and an environment where working parents do not feel that they are a problem for having children and all that family life entails.

- **Can we have affordable, better-funded childcare?**
  Childcare in the Western world is frowned upon as an
  unskilled career. It is poorly paid and shown little respect.
  This needs to change. We must recognise the care and skill
  needed in a job that literally raises the next generation and
  the roles should be properly renumerated and, importantly,
  properly funded by government. The cost of good-quality
  childcare is prohibitive for many families and the greater
  picture must be considered, with more government input.

Parenting is hard. Parenting as a working parent is particularly
hard. We must take time to recognise and appreciate the good
work we are doing, both at home and professionally. Guilt can
be crippling, and it is a huge obstacle on the path to calmer parenting. But the changes required to make life easier for working
parents are out of our hands, with the transformation needing
to take place at a societal level. Does that mean we can't do anything about our lot? I don't think so – and the next chapter is
very relevant here, as we learn how to meet our own needs and
be kinder to ourselves. Ultimately, though, what working parents
need to do is to accept that they can't do it all – and that's OK.
You are good enough, and that's all that matters.

Chapter 9

The Importance of Self-kindness – Introducing the Peaceful Pentagon

To be a good parent you need to take care of yourself so that you can have the physical and emotional energy to take care of your family.
Michelle Obama, former First Lady of the
United States of America

I always think it's insane that we often take care of our belongings better than we do ourselves. Take, for instance, those of us who have family cars: we service and MOT them, clean them inside and out (albeit not very regularly in our case), check tyre tread and oil levels, top up washer fluid and we fill them up regularly. We would never try to drive them without topping up with fuel if the needle was hovering on empty, and yet we regularly try to push ourselves when our tanks are dry. And if we did try to drive our cars without regular checks, we wouldn't blame the car if something went wrong – we would recognise that any problems were due to neglect. Yet, when we lose our cool, explode at our children or our partners or simply run out of energy and motivation to cope with the demands of parenting, we blame ourselves. We tell ourselves we're not good enough, that we are flawed, that we are not the sort of people who can be calm. We rarely stop and ask if we have taken enough care of ourselves. Isn't it crazy that we can't see what is right in front of us when we're dealing with ourselves?

One thing we must learn on the journey to calmer parenting is that resting is a necessity, not a nicety. It is a necessity to fuel body and mind if you want to be calm.

'But I don't have time for all this!'

I bet that was your first thought when you read the previous paragraph wasn't it? 'I'm already stretched thin with my children, my home, my work and other life stuff; how am I ever meant to find time to do self-care?'

And I hear you. I was like you. I used to keep on pushing forwards, however drained I felt. I simply didn't have the time to do anything for myself. That could come later when my children were older. Only it doesn't. There doesn't ever come a time where things are quieter, easier, less busy. There is never going to be a time when taking care of yourself just happens naturally. You have to make it happen.

The other thing that we must all understand is that if we don't make time to meet our own needs, we're going to have to take time to repair the disconnect, damage and dysregulation that happen when we burn out and lose our tempers at our children. Because, without taking care of ourselves we are going to be stretched so thin that we will break. It's inevitable. And we then not only have to try to meet our own needs (which are obviously increased once we're so frazzled), we also have to work to regulate our children again and resolve their problematic behaviour. Basically, clearing up the aftermath is a whole lot more time- and energy-intensive than putting in the work prophylactically.

None of us has time. Our lives are full to the brim with 'stuff' that is constantly demanding our attention, but we *must* make time. We don't need to make grand gestures. In fact, the grand gestures are the ones that so often fail because we simply can't keep them up. Instead, what we need is repeated small, positive changes. Five minutes here or there every day, rather than half a day or a whole day sporadically. The key to better meeting your needs is making it part of your everyday routine – thinking, for instance, 'I've washed the dishes and fed the pets. Have I met my own needs today?'

With this in mind, I'd like to introduce you to my Peaceful Pentagon.

The Peaceful Pentagon

The pentagon shape has long been utilised by artists to depict the perfect human form; Leonardo da Vinci's famed Vitruvian Man is one such example, with the head and both legs and arms outstretched to form the five points of the pentagon. While perfection is obviously not something I advocate striving for, I do believe that balance and peace in both body and mind is a goal that is achievable. The Peaceful Pentagon therefore focuses on the interplay between body and mind through the concepts of eating well, sleeping well, moving well, resting well and spending time in the healing properties of nature.

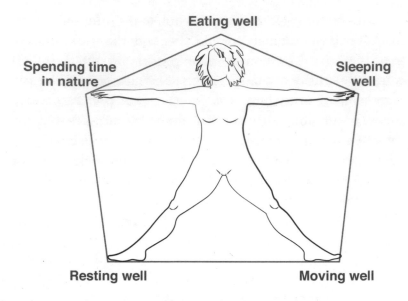

Let's look at each of the five points in some detail.

Eating well

I'm not going to start telling you what you should and shouldn't eat, give you recipes or a meal plan to follow. Mostly, because I'm not a qualified nutritionist, but also because I don't think it would help. Most of us know what we should be eating more and less of. We live in a culture that inundates us with nutrition and dieting advice. In fact, I think we would do far better with less of it because then we'd be able to eat more intuitively – or rather, we'd learn to tune out the external noise and tune in to what matters most: our own bodies.

So what should we take notice of? We would all probably do better if we could learn to recognise our own hunger and satiety cues – eating when our bodies tell us our blood sugar is getting low, choosing foods that nourish us and fuel us for longer, rather than giving us temporary spikes, and drinking when we feel the first signs of thirst. Returning to the car analogy, think of how you would top it up with fuel and fluid if it was running low, and aim to do the same with your body, learning your own unique indicators in the absence of a warning light. It would also be wonderful if we could do these things without feelings of guilt imposed on us by a society that teaches us to disconnect from our bodies and eat in a way that is far from intuitive. I won't go into detail here about eating and our relationship with food, but I do so in *The Gentle Eating Book*, if you'd like to learn more. Finally, we should be aware of any potential nutrient deficiencies we may have and how these may impact us. I would thoroughly recommend visiting your family doctor and asking for a blood test to check levels of important vitamins and minerals if you are concerned that your diet isn't optimal, and you are feeling very run down.

What parents say

I spoke to some parents about how eating and drinking impact their behaviour and relationship with their children. Here's what they told me:

> Having a toddler made me realise my behaviour also changes if I need the loo or food. Even though he's now six years old, I still make sure neither of us needs a snack or the toilet when either one of us is being irrational!

> I find it hard to be a calm parent if I am hungry! I rush around making food for everyone and then cleaning up and often forget to actually eat myself. Then I start to wonder why I am so tetchy.

> I find it hardest to stay calm when my daughter's needs (like wanting to be picked up constantly) mean I can't get the

simplest tasks – like making my morning drink – done. In those moments, I forget that she is just a toddler, and it feels personal, which of course it isn't.

I'm struggling at the moment with low vitamin D and iron deficiency. I am permanently exhausted and between trying to be a good mum, good employee, good housekeeper – I often lose it.

Sleeping well

Sleep is a thorny subject when you're a parent, especially if you have a baby or a toddler. The cruel reality is that the time in your parenting journey when you're most desperate to sleep, to recover from the gruelling exhaustion of having to meet every physical need of your child twenty-four hours per day, is the time that you're least likely to sleep, largely because of little ones needing you at night as much as they need you during the day.

For some, the answer here is sleep training babies and toddlers. Although I recognise the desperation, I don't believe that the only way to survive this period is to place all the burden of change on our children. After all, for the vast majority of babies and toddlers their sleep is entirely normal for their age, and the real problem is that it doesn't match up with adult sleep. So what do I suggest instead? I prefer to focus on sleep optimising, making sure everything is as optimal as possible in the child's life, both during the day and at night, to make their sleep as good as possible, given the limitations of their physiology and age. You're not going to get a baby or young toddler sleeping through the night in a week when you focus on optimising, but it might just help to take the edge off, so you get a little more sleep yourself. I talk more about sleep optimising in *The Gentle Sleep Book*, if you're interested in giving it a try.

Focusing on your child's sleep is only one part of the picture, though, and something I think our society is far too obsessed with. I believe, instead, it's important to look at what we can change with our own sleep, too. Most of us are doing many things wrong when it comes to sleep hygiene, and this – combined with the very normal waking of our young children – is what causes the most issues. So how can you improve your own sleep, even if you have a very wakeful child?

- **Light** For the best sleep we need lots of natural light exposure in the daytime (open blinds and curtains early in the morning and get outside in natural light as much as you can) and as little light as possible at night. In the evening draw curtains and close blinds (consider blackout blinds if there is light pollution from outside) and be mindful of light sources you use. Avoid energy-saving or fluorescent lightbulbs at night and coloured light that is blue, purple, green or similar. Any lighting you use should be on the red colour spectrum, or as close to it as possible, as this protects your body's secretion of melatonin, the hormone of sleep.
- **Screens** Following on from the previous point, limit your screen use at night, ideally, with no screen access at all for an hour before bedtime. This includes TV, tablets, laptops and mobile phones. If you must use these, then do so in 'night mode', turn the brightness down to the lowest setting or consider using a 'red light' app or wearing blue-light-filtering glasses.
- **Temperature** For the best sleep we want a cooler bedroom (that doesn't mean you can't keep warm with snuggly PJs or a thick duvet). Ideally, the room temperature will be between 15 and 19 degrees Centigrade (60 to 67 Fahrenheit). Any warmer than this and you start to inhibit the secretion of melatonin again. Also, consider sleeping with your

window open to cool the room a little and allow in some
fresh air.

- **Humidity** If the air in your bedroom is too dry, it can cause
  you to wake with a sore or dry throat. Central heating and
  air conditioning are notorious for causing this. If you do use
  either, consider investing in a humidifier or an ultrasonic
  diffuser that use water vapour. The ideal humidity level for
  sleep is around 30–60 per cent.

- **Check your pillows** Many of us tend to use too many
  pillows or pillows that are too full and firm and cause necks
  and backs to adopt a suboptimal position. Your pillow
  should support the natural curve of your spine and neck,
  leaving both in good alignment. This is more likely to
  happen if you use only one pillow.

- **Caffeine** Most people know to avoid heavily caffeinated
  drinks in the run-up to bedtime, but regularly consuming
  caffeinated drinks during the day can still impact your sleep
  negatively. The difficulty here is that we can too easily get
  into a cycle of consuming lots of caffeine because we're tired
  from poor sleep and need a pick-me-up, but the caffeine
  then contributes to poor sleep. A simple switch here is to
  make sure that at least every other drink is a glass of water.

- **Diet and exercise** We all know that a balanced diet is
  the best for us, including when it comes to sleep. Certain
  deficiencies, such as iron, magnesium and omega-3
  fatty acids, can make sleep worse, as can a suboptimal
  microbiome, with the gut flora playing a special role in
  the regulation of circadian rhythm (body clock). Similarly,
  the amount of exercise we get in the daytime impacts our
  wellbeing hugely and has a significant impact on sleep, as
  we'll discuss shortly.

- **Routine** We spend so much time trying to create the
  optimal bedtime routine for our children, then collapse
  into bed exhausted at the end of the day without a second

thought for how the same thing could help our sleep, too. Creating a simple bedtime routine for yourself – such as a warm bath or shower, followed by reading a chapter of a book, before switching off your (red) bedside lamp can really help your sleep. Another point to consider is to try to keep your sleeping times consistent, with a regular wake time and bedtime. It can be tempting to try to tank up on sleep on weekend mornings, but irregularity is the enemy of good sleep. Helping to set your circadian rhythm with regular times is much better when trying to get good-quality sleep.

One last little note here on sleep. When I consult privately with parents to help to optimise their children's sleep, I'm often given screenshot after screenshot of sleep data gained from their wearable monitors. These can be helpful if you're looking to pinpoint specific issues or working towards a fitness goal. But when it comes to sleep I find that they are usually far more anxiety-producing than helpful. Parents get incredibly hung up on the amount of sleep they've had, checking their data as soon as they wake up and stressing over nights when their devices tell them their sleep was poor, or much less than the adult average. This stress, ironically, is one of the worst enemies of sleep. Quite simply, the more stressed we are, the harder we find it to sleep. If you use a wearable monitor and you can identify yourself in this scenario, I strongly suggest you take it off at night.

What parents say

I spoke with some parents about how their sleep, or rather lack of it, impacted on their parenting. Here's what they said:

I struggle when I'm feeling drained. I will be really calm for as long as possible and then I just snap. And feel horrible about it for the rest of the day.

My resilience and patience levels are just gone when I'm tired and I can't think straight.

I struggle with tiredness . . . fatigue . . . full-on bloody exhaustion . . . When I've been up at 5.40 a.m. to do an eight-hour day in work and then I have to do the whole into-the-evening-teatime-until-bedtime routine every bloody night and I am so bloody tired, all the time and I can barely keep myself together by that point, never mind hold it together with and for my three-year-old . . . And I hate myself for feeling so resentful.

Lack of sleep is the biggest trigger for me. I can be in total control, calm and patient with my toddler when I've had enough sleep but as soon as I've had a short or disrupted night, I feel completely out of control and very extreme emotions.

Everything seems possible if I've had a good night's sleep. I'm so quick to lose my cool when I've not.

I'm not good at waking up in the morning with an alarm. But you can snooze it. I struggle when my daughter wakes up early and calls me; she has no snooze button and I have no choice but to get out of bed, usually a bit resentful.

Moving well

Do you remember when you enjoyed moving your body as a child? Back when running, jumping, skipping and dancing were joyful? Moving your body felt easy and enjoyable and sitting still all day seemed like a punishment, something to be endured. When did moving our bodies became a chore? Or something else to add to our 'to-do' list?

At some point between childhood and adulthood we lose the joy of free movement and start to view moving our bodies as 'exercise' and not simply 'fun'. Ideally, we would view movement with the same adulation as we did in childhood. The more we label moving as 'exercise', 'healthy', 'lifestyle choice' and so on, the less likely we are to want to do it.

When we become parents, our activity levels often fall, yet the more activity we undertake, the better our moods tend to be.[1] Exercise is proven to help reduce anxiety, stress and depression and helps to improve mood, by releasing the feelgood chemicals endorphins. Research has also found that parents who were more active during the Covid pandemic were likely to experience lower stress levels.[2] Moreover, research with working mothers, comparing the impact of more sleep and more exercise on overall mood, found that increased exercise had a more beneficial effect than getting more sleep.[3] One thing I have consistently found is that when I am absolutely exhausted, aching, stiff, tired, demotivated and generally feel like doing anything but exercise, that is the time I benefit from it the most. The initial push is really hard going, but if you can get through that, it will help.

We need to move away from thinking about movement in terms of losing weight and toning muscles and instead think of it as fun and a way to let off steam and stress. I have radically changed how I think about exercise in the last couple of years. Previously, I was all about slow, mindful activities, such as yoga and Pilates, because everything I read told me how good they were for staying calm. But however mindful I tried to be during a lesson, I would still run through the day's chores or demands in my mind, as I moved through the poses, and while they did help me to feel calmer temporarily, there was no real lasting impact on my mood. I've learned instead that I thrive with really loud and busy exercise, where I can throw things around, make noise and generally release any pent-up stress – all to a backing of loud and fast-paced music. For me, CrossFit, and weightlifting tick all the boxes. They feel fun – and that's the most important thing. Maybe I'll go back to the calmer movements of yoga or Pilates in the future, or maybe I'll take up something new, but the key is finding something that suits you and meets your needs at this present moment in time. So forget whatever benefits a particular type of exercise is touted as having, or what is fashionable, and just find something you enjoy. Maybe that's joining a competitive team sport for the first time since you left school; maybe it's going for a run with a friend; or maybe it's going to a roller disco, reigniting the passion for skating you had when you were eight years old. Whatever you do, try to reconnect with your inner child – the one who used to love moving their body for no reason other than it felt fun.

Resting well

What do you think of when I say the word 'rest'? Most parents would instantly say, 'What's that? I don't get time to rest!' And I would definitely have been one of them. Previously, I had two states: awake and busy or asleep. That's it. Nothing in between.

As parents, we're made to feel guilty if we rest. If we're not taking care of our children, we're working and if we're not working, we're doing housework, chores and DIY. There seems to be an unwritten rule that it is somehow lazy to rest, and busy is best, as we already discussed in Chapter 6. I hope you appreciate now that this is just not true. We need rest, just as we need air to breathe.

So what does rest look like? It instantly conjures up images of being quiet and still, but actually, the opposite could be true if it brings you clarity, space and peace. Resting could include:

- spending time alone, especially if you're feeling 'touched out'
- mindful phone and screen usage – having boundaries and screen-free time
- taking breaks from thinking about parenting – for instance, reading fiction books rather than a book like this and unsubscribing from parenting newsletters and websites and browsing something entirely unrelated
- taking up a hobby or spending leisure time doing something you enjoy
- enjoying a daytime nap
- meeting up with friends
- going for a walk
- watching a movie
- prayer
- spending time somewhere quiet, away from the noise and sensory overload of parenting
- daydreaming.

The beauty of resting is that everybody is unique, and finding what nourishes our hearts and minds is a beautiful way of reconnecting with ourselves after periods of losing sight of who we are and what we enjoy.

What parents say

I spoke to some parents and asked them why resting was so important to them, and how it affected their parenting. Here's what they said:

> I need time alone to recharge, but often, after co-sleeping, breastfeeding, being woken at dawn, having a child crying 'Mama, Mama, Mama' at me all day, even not going to the

loo alone, I just explode. It's made worse when the house is a mess and all the physical stuff feels like it's crowding in too!

I struggle if I've not had brain nourishment – reading a book, working away from home, doing something away from my toddler.

I find it so much easier to support my children with their emotions when I have had a break and I am feeling well balanced myself.

I struggle with trying to fit in time to myself somewhere . . . and the guilt that comes along with it, as it feels selfish to take an hour. I've never been berated for it, never had it held against me, it's all internal.

I struggle when there's just too much noise. Not so much the level of noise, but the number of different noises going on at once. Sensory overload.

I struggle with the fact that I just don't seem to have time to unload everything that's in my head. I miss the times when I could just relax for the day if I'd been busy at work. Sometimes I feel like I'm going to explode, but it's so hard to find time for just myself and I feel guilty if I do have it.

Spending time in nature

Nature constantly shows us how to repair and rebuild, regardless of adversity. Think of a seedling poking through a crack in a concrete pavement, or the first signs of new life after a forest fire. Nature can also reground us in times of difficulty. I'm a Taurean, an earth sign, and nothing makes me feel calmer than spending time walking barefoot among trees and plants. Sinking my feet into the earth and inhaling deeply the scents of pine needles, dew on leaves and the muskiness of the soil. If I'm angry or depleted, one of my go-tos is gardening and, as was the case for many others, the garden was my saviour during the Covid lockdowns. I understand how privileged I am to have my own garden, though. Not everyone does, and if that's the case for you, my alternative would be to find your local allotments, home-growing or rewilding community, visit a city park or local wooded area, walk alone on a nearby beach or go for a wild swim in a lake. Wherever you can find nature, embrace it, and allow it to heal your soul.

The Japanese have a word for the healing effects of spending time in a forest: shinrin-yoku or 'forest bathing'. Research has found that spending just one day in a forest significantly reduces feelings of hostility and depression and increases energy levels.[4] A further review of studies, looking at the physiological and psychological impact of forest bathing, has found that spending time in forests lowers blood pressure, heart rate and stress hormones and also reduces levels of anxiety and fatigue, while raising overall levels of emotional wellness. [5]

But spending time in nature doesn't necessarily have to mean a visit to a forest in order to benefit. It could be:

- walking to your local park
- visiting a parent-and-child forest-school session
- visiting a local nature reserve
- learning about foraging and finding local sources of wild foods
- kicking off your shoes and walking barefoot on a patch of grass.

When my children were little, my mantra used to be: 'when in doubt, go out'. When the bickering and screaming got too much,

I used to bundle us all up in warm and waterproof clothing and head for a local green space. The positive effects weren't just experienced by myself; time outdoors, in nature, always had a calming effect on my children, too. I wish now, though, that I had made my mantra 'to stop the shout, go out!' Using nature as a prophylactic, to help me to stay calm, rather than as a last resort when my calm was already wearing thin, seems a much better idea.

I think, very often, we already know what is stopping us from being calmer parents, and deep down, we already know what we need to do to help us achieve that. The only way you will have time to work on your Peaceful Pentagon is if you specifically carve it out. I hope this chapter has signalled to you that the time to do that is now!

Self-kindness: realistic and far more powerful than self-care

A couple of years ago, I decided to drop the phrase 'self-care' in favour of 'self-kindness'. I was tired of all the 'parents really must do self-care' articles that seemed to be everywhere. The idea of 'needing to do self-care' seemed to me to be another chore, something else that parents must do, another thing to add to their ever-increasing to-do list. The pressure to do self-care often set parents up for failure and guilt. Ironic, considering it is often advised as a way to ease those very things.

Instead, I now talk about self-kindness. You don't need to go anywhere, or buy anything or even carve out time for self-kindness. You can do it when you're knee-deep in nappies, toddler tantrums, dirty laundry and dinner preparations. The premise is simple: you just focus on being kinder to yourself.

You accept your flaws as entirely normal, you lower the bar with expectations of your capabilities, you forgive yourself for your mistakes and you stop comparing yourself to others (especially fictitious versions of others seen on the internet). You stop the damaging self-chatter with the three simple words: 'I am enough.' It's much simpler and far easier to keep the words 'today I will be kind to myself' in your head than it is to think, 'Eeek, I haven't done my self-care today. Another chore to add to the never-ending list.'

Have you ever stopped to think about the fact that how we treat ourselves is how our children will treat themselves? If we don't believe we are worthy of self-kindness, we will raise children who struggle with their self-esteem, no matter what we say to them. Simply, we model kindness for our children, both in the way they treat others and, as importantly, how they treat themselves. What would you want your child's self-talk to be like when they're older?

- 'I am worthy of love.'
- 'I am good enough as I am.'
- 'I like and respect myself.'
- 'It's OK for me to make mistakes; it shows I'm learning.'

Or:

- 'I don't know why anybody loves me.'
- 'I'm not good enough.'
- 'I'm useless.'
- 'I can't get anything right.'

I'm guessing that you would pick the first four examples? Yet which more closely match the thoughts you often have about yourself? If we want our children to grow with the self-kindness illustrated in the first four examples, we must speak to ourselves in that way, too. If we speak to ourselves kindly, we are more likely to model self-kindness in our own actions and behaviours, the very behaviours that our children will mimic.

How to be kind to yourself

Isn't it crazy that we need instructions on how to be kinder to ourselves? I'd bet most people could probably write their own book on how to be mean to themselves. But turn the tables and ask them how to treat themselves with empathy and respect and the ideas quickly run out. So how do you do it? Well, I'm sure you won't be surprised to hear that there are no magic solutions – just daily steps towards self-acceptance and then self-love, including the following:

- **Stop blaming yourself for 'not being calm enough'.** By now you will realise quite how much is stacked against you when it comes to parenting, and recognise the roots of the thoughts and the obstacles in your way. Your ability to be calm has very little to do with you being 'enough' of anything. It's largely situational, historical and societal. Or, in other words, it's not your fault!
- **Learn how to forgive.** What, or who, do you need to forgive in your life in order to be able to focus your future efforts on being happier and calmer and having thoughts that serve, rather than torment, you? Very often, it's ourselves, and our past misdemeanours that beg for the most forgiveness. So go ahead. Give yourself permission to forgive your mistakes. Forgive yourself for not having the knowledge you didn't have at the time. Forgive yourself for being human, just like everybody else – and feel how freeing that forgiveness is.
- **Admit when you've taken on too much.** Being busy may help to take our minds off what we perceive to be

our shortcomings and failures, but it also really tests our patience and tolerance – not just of others, but ourselves, too. Offloading chores and tasks that are non-essential (at least temporarily, if not permanently) will allow you to be calmer and, in turn, will help you to be kinder to yourself.

- **Ask for help.** Being kind to ourselves means asking for help and, most importantly, accepting help that is offered. You are worthy of help; you don't need to carry everything alone. If no help is freely offered to you, the best place to start is by telling those closest to you when you are feeling overwhelmed. We need to normalise asking for help.

- **Value your peace.** Try not to put yourself in situations that you know will stress you; for instance, avoid getting sucked into demanding debates on the internet (remember to fully utilise the block button) or drawn into arguments between two friends. If you do find yourself in such a situation, don't feel obliged to stay – instead, excuse yourself or leave quietly. Your peace is worth so much more than the desire to win an argument, especially with strangers.

- **Be comfortable with the full range of your own big feelings.** All feelings are valid and healthy; there is no such thing as 'bad feelings', even those such as anger and impatience – and you are certainly not bad for feeling them. Emodiversity is a term used to describe the importance of metaphorically sitting with all our feelings and allowing ourselves to feel them without self-judgement. The key is in how we manage these feelings. All too often, people try to drive out feelings that they deem 'negative' or somehow at odds with their quest to be calm parents, but this can be hugely counterproductive when, rather than dealing with them, they chase them away so much that they inevitably explode. Remember, again, that you are role modelling for your children at all times: what do you want them to learn about handling their own emotions? Do you want to teach them that however they feel is OK and help them to work with their emotions? Or do you want to teach them that some emotions are wrong and, as such, they are wrong for feeling them and you will give them no help in handling them? Of course, you would choose the first option for your children, and to model this mature emodiversity, you have to embrace it through your own feelings first.

- **Remember, there is a strong link between our sense of self-worth and our attempts at people pleasing.** To be kind to ourselves often means putting ourselves first, which leaves no space for people pleasing. We must work on our sense of self-worth and accept that sometimes our needs must come first. We shouldn't volunteer to do everything for others, so that they view us as a kind person – instead, we must start with the belief that we are already kind and that our kindness does not hinge on whether or not others believe we are.

I hope you can understand now why this chapter appears towards the end of the book, rather than right at the beginning. It had to come after all the chapters that talk about things affecting our ability to be kind to ourselves, including (but, of course, not limited to) our own childhoods, our tendency towards perfectionism and comparison and the impact of our busy lives and the mental as well as physical loads we carry. To be kind to ourselves means being aware of everything that we have to juggle, including the influence of others and our current and past relationships, and how these can all serve to undermine our feelings of self-worth and self-esteem. Being kind to ourselves means putting our needs front and centre, not just in spite of, but because of them.

Seven practical steps to self-kindness

So what does all this look like in practical terms? Before we move on, I want to give you a few quick exercises that can help you to move towards self-kindness. You don't have to use all of them – just pick the ones that work best for you.

EXERCISE 1: Pause and switch the voice

The next time you notice that your inner chatter is taking a negative slant, imagine pressing a big 'pause' button in your mind. Take a deep breath and imagine that the thoughts are instead coming from a parent who is well versed in self-kindness. Think about the kind and supportive messages that this calm parent would give to themselves. What sort of thing do you think they would say? Imagine that your previous negative self-chatter has been taken over by the new, calm parent. Switch the voice of your inner critic to your inner guru's and notice how the new words make you feel.

EXERCISE 2: Giving advice to others

Have you ever noticed that we are usually much kinder to other parents than we are to ourselves? I'm always amazed at the consistently wonderful supportive advice given to struggling parents in my Facebook discussion groups in comparison to the self-deprecating and disparaging posts parents write about their own parenting abilities. Imagine if we could direct that same support to ourselves that we so freely give to others. What a difference there would be. Find a quiet moment to sit and reflect on what you would say to another parent who was struggling.

Imagine that this parent confides in you that they are really battling with feelings of self-worth and confidence around their parenting abilities and that they find themselves trapped in a cycle of thinking negatively about themselves. What would you say to them to help them, not only to feel better temporarily, but to help them see that they are worthy of self-kindness and self-respect? Now imagine directing that same supportive advice to yourself.

EXERCISE 3: Celebrate your achievements

Can you remember the last time you celebrated your children's achievements? Perhaps they drew a beautiful picture, were especially kind to another child or got great marks at school. What did you say to them? Or what did you do as a family to celebrate? Now think about a time when you were celebrated for your parenting achievements. I bet you can't. Isn't it strange that we stop celebrating our achievements when we enter adulthood? Well, it's time to start again. The next time you do something you are proud of as a parent, write it down in a special 'Reasons Why I'm a Great Parent' notebook or on a small piece of card that you put in a jar. Then observe the book or jar filling up over time. You can even go back and read your notes when you're having a tough day. Or perhaps you could make yourself a 'I did great at parenting today' certificate or sticker? I've always thought, with the myriad companies making reward charts and stickers aimed at children, there is a seriously missed opportunity for those aimed specifically at parents. (**Note**: if you've read my thoughts on reward charts, stickers and certificates for children, you'll know I'm not a huge fan of them, and you may be wondering why I'm suggesting you use them yourself? Well, the reason why I'm so against them for children is because they don't look at deeper issues and their positive impact is temporary – I talk more about this in *The Gentle Discipline Book*, if you're interested. So while they're not great as a discipline technique, they can provide the perfect boost for adults who are already doing deeper work, and who just need a little pick-me-up or short-term encouragement to keep going.)

EXERCISE 4: See yourself through others' eyes

Unless you have a partner, friend or relative who is free flowing with praise about your parenting skills, it's unlikely that you have heard a compliment about them recently. We can quickly feel taken for granted, and the lack of compliments can soon erode our already fragile self-esteem. For this exercise, I'd like you to ask your partner, parent or close friend (or anybody else who you are particularly close to and knows you as a parent) to write down a list of 'Ten Reasons Why You Are a Great Parent'. When they've written it, give it a good read and let the words sink in. See how others notice the good in you more than you do yourself. Keep the list and stick it on your fridge or anywhere else you will notice it daily.

EXERCISE 5: Live authentically

Self-kindness is all about living authentically. It means that we don't put on a personality to fit in or try to change ourselves to please others. The next time you are with your friends, family, partner or even work colleagues, try to notice all the small ways in which you're inclined to clip your personality to fit in or appease others, and aim to reduce these tendencies. Instead, try to be yourself as much as possible, aim to live authentically and be the real you – you don't need to change to be liked better, but you do need to be yourself to embody self-kindness.

EXERCISE 6: Affirmations

No book about calmer parenting would be complete without some affirmations. Yes, they can seem a little clichéd, but they really do work. I spent many years working as a hypnotherapist, and the power of affirmations was always something I was in awe of. I believe they work better when you write your own, rather than read or recite those written by others. So can you think of maybe four or five positive statements about yourself, or about the you that you hope to become soon (of course, this is about changing for yourself if you want to, not for others!)? They could be as simple as, 'I am a calm parent', 'I am good enough as a parent' or, 'I show myself the same love and support as I do my children.'

When you've written a handful of positive affirmations, you need to practise reciting them to yourself. I personally feel much more comfortable reading them quietly in my head, but I know others thrive on reading them aloud each day. Try to find a minute or two at the same time each day to concentrate on your affirmations – for instance, when you finish brushing your teeth. You could always look at yourself in the mirror when you speak them, too, for added impact.

EXERCISE 7: Check your Peaceful Pentagon

Remember the Peaceful Pentagon that we discussed earlier in this chapter – the five elements we all need for calmer parenting:

1. Eating well

2. Sleeping well

3. Moving well

4. Resting well

5. Spending time in nature

Well, being kind to yourself means checking in with your Peaceful Pentagon and making sure that all five points are fulfilled. Which of these do you think you could focus on a little more? Are there any that you are already aware of neglecting?

In brief

Before we move on to the next chapter, I thought it would be a good idea to summarise the main points we have discussed about self-kindness:

- Self-kindness is far more realistic and achievable than self-care.
- Self-kindness can slot into your everyday life; it doesn't require special time or activities.
- Self-kindness is about changing our internal dialogue and making it more nurturing and supportive, in much the same way we would aim to nurture and support others, especially our children.
- So many things can impact on our ability to be kind to ourselves, such as our own upbringings. We must acknowledge this. The worst thing we can do is to berate ourselves for 'failing at self-kindness'. We must start with being mindful of the fact that for most of our lives – for one reason or another – we have been pretty mean to ourselves.
- Self-kindness means living more authentically and embracing emodiversity. All your feelings are OK; you just need to learn to accept them a little more and not berate yourself for feeling emotions often labelled as 'negative'.

When I announced I was writing this book on social media, one parent replied saying, 'Great. I just hope it's not going to just be about positive affirmations and breathing techniques.' I agreed.

In fact, I think my reply was, 'Absolutely not – being calm is definitely not that simple!' Affirmations and breathing do have their place, of course – and having just spoken about affirmations in this chapter, I'm going to mention breathing techniques in the next! They are, however, part of a much larger toolkit, and although both are useful, we need to focus on the bigger problems that need fixing before jumping in with quick-fix solutions.

I hope that this chapter has helped you to understand how self-kindness, or rather the lack of it that most parents experience, can impact on our ability to stay calm. In the next chapter, we're going to turn our focus again to a 'fix-it' mentality, as we ask: what can we do when we do inevitably struggle to be calm parents and have our own parental tantrums?

Taming the Storm and Coping in the Moment (AKA How to Not Throw Your Own Tantrums and What to Do If You Do)

There is no life that is free of pain. It's the very wrestling with our problems that can be the impetus for our growth.

Fred Rogers, American TV host

At the beginning of the book, I introduced you to my seven rules of calmer parenting. In this chapter, I want to revisit rule number two: 'Everybody loses it at times.'

My biggest worry for parents who reach this part of the book, having absorbed the information in the previous nine chapters, is that they are convinced that they can become a calm parent almost all the time. You may be wondering why on earth I would be worried about this. Surely it should be my goal? Shouldn't I want people who read my words to feel empowered and excited about the prospect of becoming calm? Absolutely, I do. I just want them to be realistic about what they can achieve – because unrealistic expectations are the cause of much pain, hurt and failure. They also cause us to give up the quest to be calmer far too soon, with a defeatist attitude and declarations that 'I'm obviously just not cut out for being a calm parent.' This isn't true. Everybody can be calmer; but nobody can be calm all (or even most) of the time.

The one thing I can tell you with certainty, no matter how much you have absorbed the messages in this book, is that you *will* lose it. You will shout at your children. You will struggle with anger and frustration. All of these are unavoidable when you are a parent. You would be inhuman if you didn't have your own tantrums. None of it makes you a bad parent. And none of this is damaging to your children either, if you do two simple things: apologise and learn from your mistakes. These two steps are what we will focus on in this chapter – or rather, how to make things right when you inevitably screw up!

Understanding the holler-and-heal cycle

In the 1970s and 1980s, American psychologist Ed Tronick was focused on working with young children and their parents, looking into the effects of something called attunement (the ability of parents to anticipate, notice and respond to their children's needs), and how this two-way interaction (the infant's communication of their needs and the parent's perception of them and their reactions) affected the child's emotional state.[1] Tronick hypothesised that the more attuned a parent–child dyad was, the better the child's emotional development would be. This positive emotional development doesn't only happen if a parent is always calm, though; children are incredibly resilient, provided a good level of attunement with their caregiver is present.

What does this mean practically? It means that it's OK to make mistakes as a parent, as long as we understand how our children feel and help them to feel better if – or, when, I should say – we upset them. This is often referred to as the rupture–repair cycle. When we inevitably lose our temper and yell at our children, we cause a rupture in our relationship with them, but our attunement with them allows us to see the hurt we have caused and leads us to repair the rupture, through holding space and containing the resulting emotions and behaviour and through gentle words and touch. I prefer to call this effect the holler-and-heal cycle – because even when I do holler and yell, I am reminded that we can still heal. I can make things right. All is not lost. Healing is always possible.

Research published in 2019 has shown that parents only need to provide a consistent, secure base or meet their children's need for attachment 50 per cent of the time, in order for them to be raised securely attached and emotionally happy.[2] I'm pretty sure, given that you're reading this book, you are already doing better than 50 per cent. In fact, I wonder if the title of this book should really be *How to Be a Calm Enough Parent*. It's surely more realistic, albeit it probably wouldn't sell as well, because we live in a society that pushes us to aim for the best, rather than 'good enough'.

How do you apologise to children?

I am always asked this when I have the holler-and-heal conversation with parents. We live in a culture where very few adults apologise to children. It's likely that we weren't apologised to during our own childhoods, especially if we were raised with a belief (held by many) that 'the adult is always right'. Only they're not.

We apologise to other adults, so why wouldn't we apologise to children? Adults mess up all the time. I actually believe it is vitally important we mess up as parents, because if we didn't, we would have no reason to apologise to our children and therefore they would never learn what to do when they make their own mistakes and need to apologise to others. It's a strange notion indeed that adults frequently force children to apologise for their misdeeds, having never been on the receiving end of an apology from an adult. How do we expect them to learn? If we want to raise children who are able to apologise – and genuinely mean what they say – we have to apologise to them. And to do that we have to screw up first.

To answer the question of how to apologise, we need to first examine what an apology is, or rather hopes to achieve. An apology is a way of admitting you made a mistake, expressing remorse and healing a relationship. Apologies, therefore, if they are to be meaningful, should be composed of three parts:

1. **Being aware of, and owning, your mistakes** This part is admitting to yourself, before you even begin to admit to your child – 'Yes, I messed up', or, 'I shouldn't have said, or done, that.'

2. **Feeling and expressing sorrow for your words or behaviour** As parents, I think we're all pretty good at feeling bad, but we often stumble over how to put that remorse into words. It can be as simple as saying, 'I'm sorry for what I said', or, 'I'm sorry I was angry at you', or, 'I'm so sorry I shouted at you.' It also helps here to acknowledge how you made your child feel, by tagging on, 'I must have really scared you', or, 'I can see how upset I made you' or, 'I made you feel sad, and I made you cry.' This acknowledgement of your child's feelings helps to validate what they are experiencing and to develop emodiversity. It also lets them know that you are aware of the consequences of your actions and that you care about their feelings.

3. **Repairing the rupture or healing the relationship after the hollering** There are no rules here – just whatever works for you and your children. Usually, a big hug is accepted well, maybe some kind words or a shared activity to rebond. If in doubt as to how you can repair the relationship, ask your child how you can make things right.

If you were raised in an environment where apologies were in short supply, it can feel uncomfortable and a little strained when you initially apologise to your children, and that's OK. Remember, you're a work in progress!

Apologies and advance notice

Sometimes we become aware of feeling wrung out and low on patience before our hollering or rupturing occurs. These are blessed moments indeed, and something that happens more often the more we work with our feelings. They allow us to give our children and our partners, friends, parents and other adults, advance notice of an impending rupture. A little like an early-alert system of a pending volcanic eruption or earthquake, only instead of seismic activity, we become aware of the internal rumbles of frustration and anger and can warn our loved ones that an eruption is imminent. This gives them a chance to give you space and gives you a chance to work on your feelings before you explode. If you can notice that your patience is hanging on by a thread, or you've had a bad day or week and can't cope with parenting right now, then the best thing you can do is to alert your children, let them know that you're struggling and ask for their grace and patience in advance. What does this look like in reality?

- 'I'm feeling really frustrated and angry today. I need some space and quiet today and I'm sorry if I shout at you.'
- 'I'm really tired and I'm struggling to cope at the moment. I just wanted to let you know in case I do explode that it's not about you and I'm sorry if I get angry. I still love you lots!'

These advance apologies and notice of impending explosions help to keep children attached and ensure attunement, even if the explosion follows. Of course, if it does, then you will still need to apologise afterwards, but you may just find that the advance notice is enough to bring about a small change in behaviour from your children to avert the impending crisis. This is more likely, of course, if your children are older, but even if they are younger, forewarning will help them to understand your emotions and realise that the difficult ones aren't a reflection of how you feel about them.

Why we must have realistic expectations of our children

I mentioned right at the beginning that this wasn't a parenting book and, as such, I haven't focused on your child's behaviour as a cause of your anger. However, I would like to cover one extremely important point that I think all parents should understand in order to be calmer – that is the fact that most of society has entirely unrealistic expectations of child behaviour.

What happens when our expectations of our child's behaviour – whether that's their sleep, their eating, their words or actions towards us or others – are unrealistic? Quite simply, we will constantly feel let down and question our parenting ability. If we demand too much of our children, expecting actions and behaviours that are not at all in line with their age and capabilities, then we 'fail' to make them behave in the desired way, and parenting is far more stressful.

Having realistic, age-appropriate, expectations of our children is so important if we want to be calmer. What do I mean here? I mean not expecting babies to sleep through the night, not expecting toddlers not to tantrum, not expecting tweenagers to be polite and not answer back and not expecting teenagers to keep their rooms tidy. Of course, this doesn't mean no discipline or boundaries in your parenting. They are important, but need to be set mindfully and in an informed way, with a good under-standing of child development and the cognitive capabilities of our children.

What parents say

I spoke with some parents about their expectations of their children's behaviour and how these influenced their ability to stay calm. Here's what they said:

> Understanding a bit about child development and things like impulse control helps to not take their behaviour personally. That helps me stay calm or calm down quickly when he presses my buttons!

> If I'm stressed because of my child's behaviour, I try to reframe it in line with their level of development and lower my expectations. Or to uncover the reasons. I'm a lot more tolerant when I can understand.

> I definitely feel less calm when I read something that makes me question what my child should be doing, but they're not. It makes me frustrated at myself for not being a good enough parent and frustrated at my child for not behaving.

Making sure your expectations of your child are age appropriate takes a lot of pressure off you as a parent, because often you'll find that when your child is doing something that you're struggling with, it's not that they are misbehaving *or* that you're making mistakes, but rather, that they are simply being a child – and that's a lot easier to empathise with.

Emotional displacement

Have you ever entirely lost it with your child over something tiny? Perhaps they refused to tidy their toys away when you asked, and yet you yelled at them as if they were a mass murderer? These moments are scary. Not just for our children, but for us, too. I'm not ashamed to say that I have scared myself several times as a parent, with a temper that was so fiery and out of control I began to wonder whether I should ever have had children, for fear of passing on to them an inability to control themselves.

What we must understand here, however, is that these moments aren't usually about us and our ability (or lack thereof) to stay calm. They don't signal some sort of epic failure as a parent either. Usually, when our reaction is totally out of proportion to something our child has said or done, we are experiencing something known as 'emotional displacement'. This occurs when our reaction is entirely over the top because it's actually about something totally different. Or, in other words, we are not actually responding to what our child has said or done, but to pent-up anxiety, worry or stress about something else, or a variety of things that have been slowly building up. The answer to this common problem is twofold:

1. Ideally, we don't let these stresses build, becoming aware of them – and, importantly, dealing with them – before

they become insurmountable. If we don't manage to do that in advance of an explosion, we quickly recognise the problem when we do explode and work hard to resolve the underlying cause afterwards.

2. We holler and heal, or rupture and repair. We apologise to our children, we comfort them and we repair and restore our relationship with them.

Emotional displacement is certainly scary, though it doesn't require a special secret solution. It requires empathy, support and understanding, not just for our children, but for ourselves, too.

Staying calm during special circumstances

When I first started to write this book, I asked many parents what they would like to see covered in it. One thing that came up several times was 'how to cope when there's a special circumstance' or an underlying difficult situation that makes it harder to stay calm. These include the following:

- Divorce or separation
- Moving house
- Changing jobs, or going back to work
- When your child is struggling with their mental health
- When you're struggling with your own mental health
- When your child makes big transitions (for example, starting school, university, etc.)
- Having unwell friends or relatives (including your children)
- Struggling with your own health
- Dealing with grief

- Having neurodivergent children (and coping with the extra challenges and judgement from others over their behaviour)
- Being a neurodivergent parent
- Having PTSD from the birth
- Parenting after previous loss (of a child)
- Struggling with hormones (for example, postnatal or premenstrual).

Of course, this isn't an exhaustive list, and I also think it's important to point out that what one parent may find challenging, another may not and vice versa.

What parents say

I spoke with several parents about their struggles to stay calm in difficult circumstances. Here's what they told me:

> I struggle because of my hormones; I've had problems forever with period pain and pre- and post-menstrual tension. I really struggle to not lash out verbally around this time and to remain engaged and calm. I think I feel much more self-doubt around this time, too. I end up having to make arrangements for me time, which means I never get any me time when I'm able to mentally enjoy it.

> I struggled with the anxiety-filled pregnancies of my living children after my first baby died. Parenting after loss added layers of stress, guilt, fear and unrealistic expectations that I needed to work on unpicking to try to let go of anger and resentment. I had to learn to manage my anxiety and to start to heal, while still honouring my grief. There's a quote that spoke to me a lot: 'I sat with my anger long enough until she told me her real name was grief.'

I struggled with PTSD from a traumatic birth experience. Any form of touch or noise overload from my environment makes the sirens go off in my head and my resilience drop through the floor.

I have chronic illnesses, so when I'm in a lot of pain or particularly fatigued I am much more easily triggered.

I'm still grieving the loss of my father and life goes on like he never existed.

I struggle most with external stresses, such as finances, house worries and work worries.

I struggle with my mum's mental health. She is often suicidal. I can't think straight, knowing I can't help her and have my own children that need me.

I struggle with losing my mum ten months ago and not having her support any more and also not having the space away from the kids to grieve.

I struggle with having a child with additional needs. Having people in public stare and judge during a meltdown is really difficult; normally I'd just try to calm him, but I almost feel pressured to tell him off.

As a single mum, I think financial issues are always a background issue that often bubbles over into stress that I can't hide around my son.

I was widowed suddenly when my son was almost three. Trying to stay calm when my emotions were all over the place and anxiety through the roof was incredibly difficult and I would often raise my voice. Sadness, lack of sleep, lack of family support and adding in pandemic restrictions meant it was a very overwhelming time. I was empty.

Being a mother with an autoimmune disease leaves me in a constant battle with exhaustion and feeling like a failure as a mother, so you try to push through, but fatigue eats away at me, then I can't meet the goals I set for myself, so I lose my calm in the frustration of it all and behave poorly and that further cements the feeling of failure.

I found parenting through my recent cancer diagnosis and treatment incredibly difficult. I was certainly far shorter tempered than usual, especially during times of scanxiety (waiting for the results of different medical scans). I have also experienced loss, raising a neurodivergent child, moving house, money worries and more. These do all undoubtedly make it a lot harder to stay calm. What can I suggest to you here? Much the same as I have suggested throughout this book:

1. Be aware of your triggers and how they affect you.

2. Ask for help or accept offers of help, if they are available.

3. Be aware of your own capabilities and do not push yourself too much. Know when to say, 'Stop, I can't take any more', and avoid 'people pleasing', so that you can focus on staying authentic and meeting your own needs.

4. Avoid comparison and quell perfectionism.

5. Work hard on self-kindness.

6. Lean on your most supportive and closest relationships and friendships or forge new ones with people who understand what you're currently going through.

7. Reset expectations of your child, so that they are age appropriate.

8. Reset expectations of yourself, based on what you are going through (it's OK to aim for getting it right only 50 per cent of the time, or even less during difficult moments).

9. Rupture and repair – recognise your mistakes, apologise to your child and make things right in the aftermath.

10. Have faith that you will get through this and stick to your goal of becoming a calmer parent. Indeed, if you can get through the darkest days, you can get through anything!

You can find some resources on page 233 that may prove helpful if you are going through any of the special circumstances that I have mentioned here.

What does the path to calmer parenting look like?

I like to compare the journey to becoming a calmer parent to one that begins with a long, dark tunnel. This tunnel is often a scary place. The tunnel is the place where we become aware of our reactions, thoughts and emotions. It is the place that often throws up painful feelings from our own childhoods – a place of repressed memories and fears. It is an incredibly uncomfortable place to spend time in, and yet we must keep moving through it, if we are to finally reach the light at the end of it. It is unavoidable if we wish to be calmer. Sometimes we may feel trapped or claustrophobic in there or we may feel like running back to the start if what we encounter is too scary to face. Sometimes we may need a push to encourage us to keep going, but we must acknowledge and face the tunnel if we ever want to emerge from it.

What happens once we're safely through the tunnel? I wish I could tell you that the work stops there, but it doesn't. No sooner are we out of the tunnel than we find out it was really the queue for a roller-coaster ride. We take a brief pause and breathe in the fresh air, feeling the warmth of the sun on our skin and then it's time for the ride to start. Maybe our roller coaster will take us through more tunnels, maybe it loops the loop, maybe it even goes into reverse. Just like life, the roller coaster keeps on going, pushing through obstacles and rising after the dips. Should we expect an easy, straight path to calmer parenting? Alas, no. Once again, if we have an expectation that it will all be easy and straightforward after some initial hard work, we will be disappointed and disorientated and we're likely to give up. But if we go in expecting the roller-coaster ride and acknowledge that the journey to becoming a calmer parent is never-ending, we have a much greater chance of sticking with it.

Calmer coping techniques

Have you ever read an article with tips on 'how to be a calmer parent'? Most likely it was full of suggestions such as 'go for a walk', 'do some meditation', or 'focus on your breathing'. These techniques can help, but they need to be acknowledged as the short-term fixes to acute situations that they are. They aren't going to do any deeper work to help you through your tunnel, or face your demons, but they may just take the edge off when you're struggling 'in the moment'. For this reason, I want to spend the rest of this chapter talking about a few techniques that have helped me. Before I do, though, here are some tips from other parents:

What parents say

I received many wonderful tips when I asked parents how they best coped when they were struggling. These are some of my favourites:

> I have a hot drink and just take that time to regather my thoughts.

> I always find that when I am present and more mindful, I'm calmer. I try to remind myself that these little humans won't be this little for ever.

> Prayer really helps me when I'm struggling to stay calm.

> I'm a long-time meditator, but I simply couldn't find time to formally sit and meditate, so I learned to take two-minute self-compassion breaks or conscious-breathing pauses. These really help me to stay calm.

> I try to spend time outdoors, with other people (when possible) and get a lie-in or afternoon snooze when I can.

> I find removing distractions and sensory inputs helps i.e. noise and light.

> I talk to my child about the big emotions I'm feeling, so he is aware that adults can get overwhelmed as well.

> I need regular time away from my responsibilities to just be me. Even five minutes a day helps me feel more centred and calmer.

> I remind myself 'don't sweat the small stuff'.

Repeating the phrase 'they didn't ask to be born' helps me as it reminds me that I am the adult and need to control *my* emotions.

I try to see me through their eyes. I don't want their adult selves looking back with lots of negative memories of me.

I always have the phrase 'pick your battles' in my head that just reminds me to have some perspective and that it probably isn't something worth stressing about.

Recognising the anger or stress helps – acknowledging it and taking five mins to do deep breaths or, even better, a quick meditation really helps me to feel calmer.

A sudden spurt of intense exercise helps to reground me and makes me think more clearly.

Every evening I take a hot shower to 'wash the day off'; I find it helps me to mentally reset.

When my young children get fussy, usually late afternoon before dinner, I put on the music speaker, and we dance to our favourite children's party songs! This literally got me through lockdown and is my go-to activity now if I feel overwhelmed.

Sometimes when I can feel myself being triggered, I like to turn it into playfulness instead to vent the frustration. Being the tickle monster and hearing them laughing or putting some music on and having a dance party usually does the trick.

Exercises – coping in the moment

As with the previous chapters, I want to give you several action-able and practical exercises you can use, this time with a focus on staying calm during the storm of big, difficult feelings – both yours and those of your children. The key to using any exercise during times of heightened emotions is to practise it when you are calm. If you are used to a technique and can do it with ease during times of stillness and rest, it is much more likely that it will work when you are stressed and struggling.

EXERCISE 1: Five bands

Wear five red bands (elastic hairbands work well) on your right wrist. Each time you override your anger when responding to your child move a band to your left hand. Your goal is to have all five bands on your left wrist by the end of the day, but any at all on your left hand is cause for celebration!

EXERCISE 2: Visit your calming place

Close your eyes and picture yourself in your favourite place; it could be a beach, a forest, a mountain – wherever you feel calm, happy and relaxed. Take yourself off there for a minute or two when you're most in need of peace.

EXERCISE 3: Wear a calm suit

Picture somebody who always seems calm and relaxed. Imagine stepping inside their body and wearing it as a suit. Feel how calm they are and let the peace soak into your own body. Think about how they might respond to situations that trigger your anger.

EXERCISE 4: Let it out

Call a friend or have a good rant on an internet discussion group. My Gentle Parenting group on Facebook is full of kind and non-judgemental parents who will listen to you (see Resources, page 233).

EXERCISE 5: Time out

Take a parental 'time out'. If it is safe, leave your children and spend a minute or two alone in a room, until you feel a little calmer.

EXERCISE 6: Get outside

It doesn't matter what the weather is like – throw on a heavy winter coat or raincoat or dig out your sunhat and shades and get outside for a walk for ten minutes. Breathe in the fresh air and feel the sun, rain or snow on your skin.

EXERCISE 7: Get moving

Pop on your trainers and go for a run, turn on the radio or put the TV on a dance channel and dance around your kitchen to music. Just move and feel your frustrations leaving your body with each pound of your feet or shake of your arms or hips.

EXERCISE 8: Yell it out

Take yourself somewhere private and have a good old scream to release the tension.

EXERCISE 9: Hug it out

Give your children, or your partner, or even a childhood teddy bear a big squeeze and feel the relaxing effects of the oxytocin you release.

EXERCISE 10: I-spy senses

Find five things you can see right now, then four different things you can touch, three different things you can hear, two you can smell and, finally, one thing you can taste right now to centre yourself in the present moment.

EXERCISE 11: Clean it out

Take your tensions out on your dirty dishes, grubby skirting boards or greasy oven. The bonus here is that not only do you come out of it calmer, but with a cleaner home, too!

EXERCISE 12: Cry it out

No, not a misguided attempt to get a baby to sleep! Having a good cry when we're stressed not only helps to release pent-up emotions, but also to release cortisol, the stress hormone, through our tears. Crying is incredibly healing.

Maybe you have your own unique way to feel calmer in moments of stress? The beauty of finding your own techniques is that they often become family traditions, passed down through generations as healthy ways to deal with difficult emotions. So whatever technique you use, it's not only helpful for you, but also your children. Because even in times of stress, we are still teaching our children – and arguably, nothing could be more valuable to them than watching us successfully manage our own big emotions, because that, ultimately, is how they learn to manage their own.

In brief

Here's a summary of the most important points we have covered in this chapter regarding tackling our own tantrums as parents and how to repair any damage we may cause:

- All parents mess up. All parents have their own tantrums. Losing your temper is unavoidable. It is inevitable and you shouldn't feel like a failure when it happens.
- Parents who are well attuned to their children – who show gentle, nurturing, supportive parenting, with empathy and respect – protect their children against any mistakes they make. We only need to be 'good enough' and get it right 50 per cent of the time to raise emotionally healthy, well-attached children.
- When we lose our tempers and yell, we cause a rupture in our relationship with our children; however, we can repair it – it is not broken forever. Once we have hollered, it is time to focus on healing.
- We repair our relationships by apologising to our children and making things right. This starts with acknowledging our mistakes.
- It's important that we mess up as parents, otherwise our children won't know how to repair a rupture or make an honest apology. These difficult times are learning moments for our children, as well as for us as parents.
- The journey to becoming a calmer parent can feel scary, like going through a long, dark tunnel. We may be tempted to abandon our journey or give up and run back to the start

when it feels too difficult, but light is on the other side if we can keep going.

- Even when we're through our tunnel and it is easier to be calmer, we are still on a roller-coaster ride, with ups and downs and unexpected turns. Becoming calmer is a never-ending journey. There will always be something to challenge us, and that's OK – we just need to recognise that when we hit the troughs instead of the peaks this is life, not something we have done wrong.

I want to end this chapter with a quote from a famous and very wise philosopher – Big Bird from *Sesame Street* – who said, 'Bad days happen to everyone, but when one happens to you, just keep doing your best and never let a bad day make you feel bad about yourself.'

My aims with this chapter were threefold: 1. To help you recognise that *all* parents mess up; you are not unique in your struggles. 2. To help you understand that messing up is not the end of the story; children are resilient, and can cope with our mistakes – in fact, they even learn from them. And, finally, 3. To help you accept that you are a *great* parent, even though I suspect you don't feel like one. It really is time for you to stop feeling bad about yourself and put what you have learned here into practice. I have every faith that you can do it.

Chapter 11

The Seven Golden Rules of Calmer Parenting – a Refresher and a Closing Note

I want to end this book with a recap of my Seven Golden Rules of Calmer Parenting, as a final reminder before you go on your way. I hope that now, with the knowledge you have gained from Chapters 1–10, these rules will speak to you with a little more clarity and meaning. Perhaps there is one that speaks to you a little more loudly? Or one that you feel is more in line with where you are in your life and parenting right now? Anyway, here are the Seven Golden Rules of Calmer Parenting:

1. **Everybody can be a calmer parent.** It doesn't take any special personality traits. Privilege does inevitably mean that life is infinitely easier for some, but we can *all* do some work and make some changes that will have a positive impact, regardless of our life situations.

2. **Everybody loses it at times.** Nobody is calm 100 per cent of the time – nobody should aim to be. We must lower the bar when it comes to expectations of what we can achieve, and we must not compare our 'inner selves' (our innermost thoughts and feelings) with the 'outer selves' (the carefully curated illusions) of others. You're

not alone. All parents act in ways they're ashamed of. Everybody has to try hard to hold it together. Losing your temper doesn't mean you're not good enough or lack willpower, and it definitely doesn't make you a worse parent than somebody else.

3. **It is not your fault that you aren't a calm parent.** Read that again and stop blaming yourself. Parents carry such a burden of guilt and instantly blame themselves when they are angry and short-tempered with their children. But it isn't your fault; we are who we are due to the way we were raised, the situations we find ourselves in and the relationships we have with others. Don't think 'what's wrong with me?' Instead, see yourself as a combination of things that have happened to you and the environment you are in – you are not flawed. And the good news is that you can assert some control over how you process these experiences and the hold they have on you in the future.

4. **You are still going to have lots of big feelings.** You are not aiming to get rid of the big feelings, just to cope with them in a healthier way. You will still feel anger, frustration, worry and disappointment, in both yourself and your children – and that's OK. All feelings are OK. In short, the key to being calmer is allowing and accepting these big feelings and turning reactivity into responsivity: putting a space between your child's actions, your feelings and your response. Becoming calmer is about self-awareness, self-acceptance and self-forgiveness, not trying to turn yourself into some sort of emotionally devoid robot.

5. **Messing up doesn't undo all the good you've done before.** A bad day is simply that – a bad day. It does not

make you a bad person or a failure. Even if that day stretches into weeks, months or years. It doesn't undo the work you have previously put in to becoming calmer or cancel out the good days. It also doesn't have any impact on what you can achieve in the future. The road to calmer parenting is full of ups and downs – you will mess up, you will feel like you've taken a million steps back some days – but you just need to keep going and accept the topsy-turvy route to progress. Real life is messy and so is real change.

6. **The journey to becoming calmer takes time**. Make sure your goals are realistic, you're not going to change overnight, or even in a month or two. You are going to be a work in progress for pretty much the rest of your life – and that's OK, because even a tiny change is still a change. Although it may sound terribly clichéd, a thousand tiny steps will get you further than one giant leap. Commitment and consistency are key; repeated small changes are better than one-off attempts at enormous change.

7. **You will not screw up your child when you 'lose it'.** This is maybe the most important rule to really and truly assimilate because the guilt we carry with us when we screw up can have such a damaging effect on our future attempts. Children are resilient, and our mistakes as parents help them to grow. What matters more is how you repair any rift that happens afterwards. Knowing how to heal the hurt caused during our inevitable 'uncalm' moments is part of the foundation of calmer parenting. So too is learning to palliate any feelings of inadequacy and guilt that accompany them, to turn them into something productive instead.

Throughout this book we have looked at different areas of our lives, both past and present, that impact on our ability to be calm. In the previous chapter, I introduced you to some ways that you could be calmer 'in the moment', when you feel as if you are losing control. The key to calmer parenting, however, is in understanding the triggers and problems that stop us being calm in the first place. It's great to have some coping mechanisms, but we must work to uncover the root causes and obstacles in our path if we want to make real change to the way we parent.

Completing your calm parenting jigsaw puzzle

Being calm is like a jigsaw puzzle. You can't complete the jigsaw with one piece alone. There are no quick fixes, only dogged, determined work and a huge heap of patience. To complete a jigsaw, you must first make sure all the pieces are in the box. The path to calmer parenting follows the same process: first we investigate the contents of our box and check the pieces, locating the most important ones as a starting point. Then it's a case of looking carefully at each of the remaining pieces, turning them the right way up and slotting them in one by one. You can use the visual of the jigsaw puzzle to help you on your path to calmer parenting.

Very often, when parents are struggling with staying calm, and when they're struggling with difficult behaviour from their children, it's because they have forgotten a missing piece of their calmer-parenting puzzle. Do bookmark this page and come back to the calmer-parenting jigsaw puzzle if you find yourself struggling in the future. You could even draw your own and colour in each part as you feel your work is complete – it's a great way to monitor your progress, and also to note that just as the colours don't disappear if you slip up, losing your cool now and again doesn't undo all the hard work and time you have put into the pieces and the puzzle overall.

THE SIX SECRETS OF STAYING CALMER

As you may have realised, especially if you have read my other parenting books, I do love an acronym to help me retain instructions and important information! The acronym CALMER might help you to remember the secrets of staying calmer as a parent:

Censor thoughts of self-doubt, self-criticism, comparison and self-sabotage – you can do this. You can be a calmer parent!

Accept yourself unconditionally for all that you are and understand how your past has influenced you. It is not your fault that you are not always calm. You are not a bad parent.

Live in the moment. Becoming calmer means being aware of how your past influences the present, but it doesn't mean living there or dwelling on it. Living in the moment helps you to be mindful and focus on your current behaviour and actions. It also helps you to be aware of your needs.

Master one or two 'go-to' responses to help you cope in the moment, making them a habit to turn to if you're struggling. Any coping strategies should be well-practised, so they are second nature to you.

Empty your container. What do you need to do to make space in your container, so that you are less likely to erupt or have your own tantrum as a parent?

Reflect on what has happened after you lose your cool. What can you learn from it? What did you do well? What can you do better next time? View mistakes as an opportunity to learn. Don't dwell on the guilt; pick yourself up and start again. We are all works in progress!

A closing note

I want to close this book with a thank you: thank you for trusting me to help you on this journey. I am deeply honoured. I have worked with thousands of people to help them become calmer, happier parents, and it is something I never tire of. Knowing that the work doesn't just transform your life but those of your children and future grandchildren, too, is thrilling.

I know the stress, worry, anxiety, guilt, pain and overwhelming feelings of inadequacy that accompany parenting. I know what it's like to feel wrung out and out of control, and they are not feelings I would wish on anyone. I also know the peace that accompanies understanding your triggers, meeting your own needs and, finally, *finally* being kind to yourself as a parent, after months, or often years of admonishing and beating yourself up over your perceived failures.

Just like me, you deserve to be happy, and you deserve to be calmer as a parent. A lot of people think I'm some sort of zen guru. I am not. I'm just a parent who has had to deal with a lot of stuff life threw at her. I'm no better than you. I'm just a little further ahead of you on my journey, and I have every faith that you can join me on the path to becoming a calmer parent, too.

Sarah

References

Chapter 1

1 Freud, S. 'Neurosis and psychosis', SE, 19 (1924), pp. 149–153.
2 Felitti, V. J., Anda, R. F., Nordenberg, D., et al., 'Relationship of childhood abuse and household dysfunction to many of the leading causes of death in adults. The Adverse Childhood Experiences (ACE) Study', *American Journal of Preventive Medicine*, 14(4) (1998), pp. 245–58.
3 Porges, S., (2009), 'The polyvagal theory: new insights into adaptive reactions of the autonomic nervous system', *Cleveland Clinic Journal of Medicine*, 76 (Suppl 2) (2009), pp. 86–90.

Chapter 2

1 Robinson, A., Abramovitch, A., (2020), 'A Neuropsychological Investigation of Perfectionism', *Behavior Therapy*, May;51(3):488–502; Stoeber, J. and Otto, K., 'Positive conceptions of perfectionism: approaches, evidence, challenges', *Personality and Social Psychology Review*, 10(4) (2006), pp. 295–319; Segrin, C., et al., 'Overparenting is associated with perfectionism in parents of young adults', *Couple and Family Psychology: Research and Practice*, 9(3) (2020), p. 181.
2 Azizia, K. and Besharat, M., 'The relationship between parental perfectionism and child perfectionism in a sample of Iranian families', *Procedia Social and Behavioral Sciences*, 15 (2011), pp. 1287–90.

3 Hewitt, P. L. and Flett, G. L., 'Perfectionism in the self and social contexts: Conceptualization, assessment, and association with psychopathology', *Journal of Personality and Social Psychology*, 60 (1991), pp. 456–70.

4 Sorkkila, M. and Aunola, K., 'Risk Factors for Parental Burnout among Finnish Parents: The Role of Socially Prescribed Perfectionism', *Journal of Child and Family Studies*, 29 (2020), pp. 648–59.

5 Woodhouse, S., Scott, J., et al., 'Secure Base Provision: A New Approach to Examining Links Between Maternal Caregiving and Infant Attachment', *Child Development*, 91(1) (2019), pp. 249–65.

Chapter 3

1 Summerville, A. and Roese, N., 'Dare to Compare: Fact-Based versus Simulation-Based Comparison in Daily Life', *Journal of Experimental Social Psychology*, 44(3) (2008), pp. 664–71.

2 Zhang, M., Zhang, Y. and Kong, Y. 'Interaction between social pain and physical pain', *Brain Science Advances*, 5(4) (2019), pp. 265–73.

3 White, J. and Langer, E., 'Frequent Social Comparisons and Destructive Emotions and Behaviors: The Dark Side of Social Comparisons', *Journal of Adult Development*, vol. 13, no. 1 (2006).

4 Festinger., L., 'A theory of social comparison processes', *Human Relations*, 7(2) (1954), pp. 117–40.

5 Thai, S., Lockwood, P., et al., 'The family ties that protect: Expanded-self comparisons in parent–child relationships', *Journal of Social and Personal Relationships*, 36(3) (2019), pp. 1041–66.

6 Deri, S., Davidai, S. and Gilovich, T., 'Home alone: Why people believe others' social lives are richer than their own', *Journal of Personality and Social Psychology*, 113(6) (2017), pp. 858–77.

7 Park, S. and Baek, Y., 'Two faces of social comparison on Facebook: The interplay between social comparison orientation, emotions, and psychological well-being', *Computers in Human Behavior*, vol. 79 (2018), pp. 83–93.

Chapter 4

1 Maslach, C., 'Burned-Out', *Human Relations*, 9(5) (1976), pp. 16–22.
2 Horne, R. M., Johnson, M. D., Galambos, N. L. and Krahn, H. J., 'Time, Money, or Gender? Predictors of the Division of Household Labour Across Life Stages', *Sex Roles*, 2017.
3 Ahn, J. N., Haines, E. L. and Mason, M. F., 'Gender Stereotypes and the Coordination of Mnemonic Work within Heterosexual Couples: Romantic Partners Manage their Daily To-Dos', *Sex Roles*, 77 (2017).
4 Brewster, M. E., 'Lesbian women and household labor division: a systematic review of scholarly research from 2000 to 2015', *Journal of Lesbian Studies*, 21 (2017), pp. 47–69.
5 Moberg, Y., 'Does the gender composition in couples matter for the division of labor after childbirth?' Working Paper Series 8 (2016), IFAU – Institute for Evaluation of Labour Market and Education Policy.
6 Office for National Statistics, 'Families and Households in the UK: 2020', retrieved 4 August 2021.
7 'The Majority of Children Live With Two Parents, Census Bureau Reports', United States Census Bureau, 17 November 2016, retrieved 4 August 2021.

Chapter 6

1 Adams, G., Converse, B., Hales, A. and Klotz, L., 'People systematically overlook subtractive changes', *Nature*, 592 (7853), 2021.

Chapter 7

1 Lippold, M. A., Glatz, T. and Fosco, G., 'Parental Perceived Control and Social Support: Linkages to Change in Parenting Behaviors During Early Adolescence', *Family Process,* 57(2) (June 2018), pp. 432–47.
2 Thomas, P., Liu, H. and Umberson, D., 'Family Relationships and Wellbeing', *Innovations in Aging*, 1(3) (November 2017).

3 Doss, B., Rhoades, G., Stanley, S. and Markman, H., 'The effect of the transition to parenthood on relationship quality: an 8-year prospective study', *Journal of Personality and Social Psychology*, 96(3) (2009), pp. 601–19.

Chapter 8

1 Ellison, G., Barker, A. and Kulasuriya, T., 'Work and Care: A Study of Modern Parents', Equality and Human Rights Commission, YouGov Research Report: 15 (2009).
2 Cleo (2020), 'State of Working Parents Survey', Q3: https://hicleo. com/resource/the-state-of-working-parents-study-q3-2020/
3 Promundo: 'Helping Dads Care' report, accessed online 17 August 2021; https://promundoglobal.org/wp-content/ uploads/2018/06/Promundo-DMC-Helping-Men-Care-Report_ FINAL.pdf

Chapter 9

1 Limbers, C., McCollum, C. and Ylitalo, K., 'Physical activity in working mothers: Running low impacts quality of life', *Women's Health*, vol. 16 (2020), p. 20.
2 Limbers, C., McCollum, C. and Greenwood, E., 'Physical activity moderates the association between parenting stress and quality of life in working mothers during the Covid-19 pandemic', *Mental Health and Physical Activity* (October 2020), p. 19.
3 Fortier, M., Guerin, E. and Williams, T., 'Should I exercise or sleep to feel better? A daily analysis with physically active working mothers', *Mental Health and Physical Activity* (March 2015), pp. 56–61.
4 Morita, E., Fukuda, S., Nagano, J., et al., 'Psychological effects of forest environments on healthy adults: Shinrin-yoku (forest-air bathing, walking) as a possible method of stress reduction', *Public Health*, 121(1) (January 2007), pp. 54–63.
5 Li, Q., 'Effets des forêts et des bains de forêt (shinrin-yoku) sur la santé humaine: une revue de la littérature [Effects of forest bathing (shinrin-yoku) on human health: A review of the literature]', *Sante Publique*, S1(HS) (13 May 2019), pp. 135–43.

Chapter 10

1 Tronick, E., 'Emotions and Emotional Communication in Infants', *American Psychologist*, vol. 44(2) (1989), pp. 112–19.
2 Woodhouse, S., Scott, J., Hepworth, A., et al., 'Secure Base Provision: A New Approach to Examining Links Between Maternal Caregiving and Infant Attachment', *Child Development*, 91(1) (January 2020), e249–e265.

Resources

Sarah's website: www.sarahockwell-smith.com
Sarah's Facebook: www.facebook.com/sarahockwellsmithauthor
Sarah's Instagram: www.instagram.com/sarahockwellsmith
Sarah's YouTube: www.youtube.com/c/sarahockwellsmith
Sarah's Twitter: www.twitter.com/thebabyexpert

Chapter 1

How to cope with a difficult parent: www.myhorridparent.com
Mental-health support: www.mind.org.uk
How to find a therapist: www.bacp.co.uk
Inner-child work: www.ppfoundation.org

Chapter 2

Perfectionism scale questionnaire: https://hewittlab.psych.ubc.ca/measures-3/
                                      perfectionism-ratings-scale/

Chapter 7

Relationship advice and support:	www.relate.org.uk
	www.gottman.com
Advice for those in an abusive relationship:	www.nationaldahelpline.org.uk
	www.womensaid.org.uk
Bereavement support:	www.cruse.org.uk
Motherless mothers:	www.hopeedelman.com
Gentle Parenting UK Facebook group:	www.facebook.com/groups/GentleParentingUK
Gentle Parenting International Facebook group:	www.facebook.com/groups/GentleParentingInternational

Chapter 10

Parenting through cancer:	www.mummystar.org
	www.macmillan.org.uk
	www.maggies.org
Single parenting/ parenting through separation:	www.gingerbread.org.uk
Parenting through mental-health struggles:	www.mind.org.uk
Parenting children with mental-health struggles:	www.youngminds.org.uk
Parenting through grief:	www.winstonswish.org
Parenting children with serious illness:	www.rainbowtrust.org.uk
Parenting neurodivergent children:	www.adhdfoundation.org.uk
	www.autism.org.uk
Parenting through birth trauma:	www.birthtraumaassociation.org.uk
Parenting after previous child loss:	www.tommys.org
Support for parents with money worries:	www.citizensadvice.org.uk

Index

Note: page numbers in *italics* refer to diagrams, pages numbers in **bold** refer to information contained in tables.

abuse
    domestic 21
    see also childhood abuse
acceptance
    and life transitions 110
    of the self 41, 225
    and social comparison-making
        71
    see also self-acceptance
ACE *see* adverse childhood
    experience
achievements, celebration of
    194–5
adaptability 99, 100–16
addiction 21
additional needs children 209
additive behaviours 119
adrenal glands 23
adrenaline 23
adverse childhood experience
    (ACE) 12–15, 17–22
    healing from 29–31
    impact on development 22
    types of 20–1
advertising 49

advice
    giving 193–4
    unsolicited 144–8
affirmations, positive 57, 196–7
alcoholism 21
altruism 140
Angelou, Maya 157
anger 1–3
    and busy lifestyles 118
    and coping in the moment 200,
        204, 208
    and the five bands exercise
        215
    and the mental and physical
        load of parenting 79
    recognition 214
anxiety 1, 3, 226
    and coping in the moment 208,
        210
    and life transitions 107
    and the mental and physical
        load of parenting 80
    and perfectionism 47
    and physical exercise 183
    post-birth 103

social 137
and social comparison-making 74
and spending time in nature 187
and unsolicited parenting advice 144
apologies
in advance 203–4
to children 201–4, 207
how children learn to make 55, 202–3
arguments 153, 191
attachment, secure 201
attention-seeking behaviour 49
attunement 200–1, 218
authentic living 195, 197
authoritarian parents 25
autoimmune diseases 210
avoidance behaviours 58, 191

babies 101–3
barefoot walking 187
bedtime routines, for parents 180–1
beliefs 37–8, 71–2
see also self-belief
bereavement 208, 209–10
Big Bird (Sesame Street character) 219
Bion, Wilfred 96
black-and-white thinking 59
blame
parent-blaming 15
see also self-blame
blood pressure 187
blood sugar levels 176–7
body scan meditation 35–6
boredom, benefits of 125–6, 128, 129, 131
boundary setting 123–5, 164–5
breaks, taking 75, 163, 165, 168–9, 185, 216
breathing techniques 38, 197–8

diaphragmatic (belly) breathing 28
Brown, Brene 75
Brownn, Eleanor 61
bucket model of stress 19–20, 20
bullet lists 111
burnout 25
awareness of the symptoms of 91, 99
and being honest with yourself 92
and busy lifestyles 118, 130
cynicism of 77, 78
depersonalisation of 77
and the division of parental chores 79, 82
emotional 77–8
and life transitions 106
and lightening the load 75, 77–8, 90–8
and the mental and physical load of parenting 75, 77–8, 89–99
and people-pleasing 139
and perfectionism 46, 52
physical 77
and self-employment 164–5
and single parents 89
busy lifestyles
disadvantages of 8, 117–31
and the mental and physical load of parenting 79–81
and overscheduled children 127–8, 131
and realising you have taken on too much 190–1
rewarding 118–19
and self-kindness 190–1

caffeine 180
calm parenting 1–9
and the art of doing nothing 8, 117–31

and busy lifestyles 8, 117–31
during difficult situations
        207–11
jigsaw puzzle metaphor of
        223–4, *224*
and life transitions 8, 100–16
long-term process of 6, 222
and the mental and physical
        load of parenting 8, 75–99
and parental childhood
        experience 5, 7, 11–42
and parenting perfectionism
        7–8, 42, 43–60
path to 211–12
and present moment coping 9,
        199–219
and relationships 8, 132–56
and self-kindness 9, 172,
        173–98
and setbacks 6, 221–2
seven golden rules of 4–7,
        220–6
and the six secrets of staying
        calmer 225
and social comparison-making
        8, **33**, 60, 61–74
and work–life balance 9, 157–70
calm suits (exercise) 215
calming places, visualisation 215
cancer 1–2, 210
cars **87**
catecholamines 23
celebrations **85**
change *see* life transitions
child development 204–6, 211
CHILD technique 29–30
childbirth, traumatic 209
childcare
    and Covid-19 170
    undervalued nature of 49
    and work-life balance 162–3,
        172

childhood abuse
    emotional 20
    and the fawn response 25
    mental 142
    physical 21, 142
    sexual 21
    verbal 20
childhood experience
    adverse (ACE) 12–15, 17, 18–22,
        29–31
    effects of 5, 7, 11–42
    exercises to deal with 31–9
    healing from 29–31
    and perfectionism 47–9
    and the polyvagal theory 27–9
    and revisiting childhood
        memories 56
    talking to your own parents
        about your 40
    talking to your parents about 40
chores, gender inequality in the
        division of 78–82, **83–8**, 90,
        92, 98
chunking 112
circadian rhythms 181
cleaning **83**, 217
clothing, children's **85**
co-dependency 142
cognitive dissonance 145, 146
cold exposure technique 28
communication skills 152, 154–6
commuting 167–8, 169
comparison-making *see* social
        comparison-making
conception, difficulties with 103
confidence 45, 47
conflict avoidance 25, **32**
connection 110, 127, 134–5
conscious mind 16–17, *16*, 29
consumerism 49
containment, emotional 96, 99,
        201, 225

control issues 3–4, **33**, 100, 109, 142

coping 225
  calmer 212–14
  with the guilt of being a working parent 161–2
  lying about our ability to 92
  see also present moment coping

cortisol 217

counselling 151

Covid-19 pandemic 2, 100, 101
  and doing less 120–1
  and the mental and physical load of parenting 80
  and physical exercise 183
  and relationships 134–5
  and spending time in nature 187
  and transition 106
  and working from home 169–70
  see also lockdowns

cranial nerve 27–8

critical people 46, 144–8
  turning criticism into compliments 37
  see also self-criticism

crying 18, 217

dancing 214

daylight 179

deadlines, difficulty meeting 47

delegation 46, 94–5, 191

demons, parental 3

Demsetz, Harold 45

dependency 142

depression
  and perfectionism 44, 47
  and physical exercise 183
  and spending time in nature 187

diaphragmatic (belly) breathing 28

diet 176–8, *176*, 180

difference, respecting 152–3

difficult situations, staying calm in 207–11

disagreements 152–3

discipline
  authoritarian **34**
  distraction methods **34**
  gentle 150
  and reward charts 194–5

disconnect 134–5

disrespect 17, 18

dissatisfaction, general sense of 46

distraction methods **34**

divorce 21

doing nothing, art of 8, 117–31
  allocating time to 128
  and the benefits of boredom 125–6, 128–9, 131
  and boundary setting 123–5
  challenges and exercises 128–30
  and the creation of simple memories 127–8
  noting the effects of 130
  and the power of play 122–3, 129
  when less is more 119–21, 130

domestic abuse 21

drug addiction 21

dyad, parent–child 200

eating well 176–8, *176*, 180

elephants 133–4

emotional abuse 20

emotional burnout 77–8

emotional containment 96, 99, 201, 225

emotional displacement 206–7

emotional neglect 21

emotional regulation
  failure to learn 19
  inhibition 11–12
  lack of parental 4

emotional release 97–8, 216
emotional repression 13, 18–19
  being taught 93
  breakdown of 19–20, *20*
  and fear of vulnerability **34**
  letting go of 29, 30
  and perfectionism 48
  and toxic positivity 65
emotional wellness 187
emotions
  authentic 29–30
  big 6, 19, 97, 213, 221
  and the fawn response 25
  letting go of 29
  parents' abilities to contain
    their children's 96
  and self-kindness 191–2
  and unsolicited advice 145
  bottling up *see* emotional
    repression
  children made to feel
    responsible for their
    parents' 12–13
  containment 96, 99, 201, 225
  difficult 96, 133
  honouring your 29–30
  letter-writing about your 154–5
  and perfectionism 45–6
  and relationships 133
  unresolved 2
empathy
  being treated with 12
  and relationships 156
  and social comparison-making
    63
  and toxic positivity 65
  for your own parents 15
  see also self-empathy
endorphins 183
entertainment **88**, 121, 125
  over-entertainment 127–8
exhaustion 143

and the mental and physical
    load of parenting 75, 77–8
  and nutrient deficiencies 178
  and physical exercise 183
  and sleep 178, 182
  see also burnout; tiredness
expectations
  about children's behaviour
    204–6, 211
  and life transitions 110
  lowering the bar regarding 189
  of parenthood 103
  and perfectionism 44–6, 50–3,
    58
  and self-kindness 189
  unrealistic 199
  and working parents 161, 166
extended families 90

failure
  embracing 43–60
  fear of 58
  reframing 57
  value of 54–5
families **87**
  critical 143
  entertainment **88**
  extended 90
  lack of support from 135, 150–1
  who make you feel bad about
    your parenting abilities
    143–8
fatherhood
  and burnout 77
  transition to 103
favouritism **33**
fawn response 23–7, 46–7, 139
fear
  of failure 58
  and life transition 107
  of vulnerability **34**
feelings *see* emotions

Festinger, Leon 66
fight response 23–9, 46–7
five bands exercise 215
Flett, Gordon 50
flexibility 99, 100–16
flight response 23–7, **34**, 46–7,
    130
food preparation **83**
forest bathing 187
forgiveness
    of our own parents 30–1
    see also self-forgiveness
fourth trimester 103, 164
freeze response 24, 27, 46, 47
Freud, Sigmund 15–17, *16*
Freudenberger, Herbert 77
friendships **87**
    feeling unpopular 139–40
    making friends as an adult
        136–7
    moving on from 138
    supportive 210
    that make you feel bad about
        your parenting abilities
        143–8
    toxic 138
frustration 79–80, 200, 204
funerals 113

garden maintenance **86**
gay men 78–9
gender stereotypes 78
'getting your crap together' 3
gifting **85**
Glatz, Terese 134
goals
    chunking 112
    and comparison-making 64
    and life transitions 112
    realistic 6, 58–9
    unobtainable 48
'good' (compliant) children 12, 32

'good enough', feeling, and social
    comparison-making 61–3, 64,
    68, 69
'good-enough' parenting 53–60
    feeling like you can't achieve
        43–4
    and the load of parenting 89
    moving towards 56–9
grandparents 30–1, 40, 143
gratitude 65
grey zone, the 59
grief, staying calm through 208,
    209–10
grocery shopping **83**
guilt 1, 4–7, 221–2, 226
    and doing nothing 117
    and eating 177
    getting rid of 43–60
    and goal-setting 112
    and the mental and physical
        load of parenting 79
    and perfectionism 44–5
    and resting 184, 186
    toxic 8
    and working parents 158,
        159–62
Gupta, Masaba 43
gut bacteria 180

'having it all' 9
headspace 45, 57, 78, 95–6, 111,
    167–8
helicopter parenting 47, 49
help, asking for 17–18, 89, 92–5,
    191
helping others 139–40
Hewitt, Paul 50
high achievers 48, 49, 50
holiday planning **86**
holler and heal cycle (rupture–
    repair cycle) 7, 9, 200–1, 207,
    211

home maintenance **86**
home working 121, 169–70
honesty 92
household finance management
   84
housework **83**
hugging it out (exercise) 217
humidity 180
hunger 176–7
hypervigilance 47, 59

I-spy senses (exercise) 217
identity loss 167
illness, staying calm through 209,
   210
independence 53, 55, 93
indignation, parental **32**
inner child, healing 13–15, 29–39
inner dialogue/talk 12
   children's 189–90
   imagining that of others 58
   pausing and switching 193
   and perfectionism 45, 50–1, 58
   and self-kindness 193, 197
   and social comparison-making
      70
inner experience 14
inner self 5, 220
insecurity 49
isolation 97–8

journaling 112
Jung, Carl 17

Kabat-Zinn, Jon 116

labyrinth art 114–15, *115*
Leonardo da Vinci 175
lesbians 78–9
letter-writing
   and relationships 154–5
   to the past you 36

letting it out 97–8, 216
life transitions (change) ·8, 100–16
   achieving personal 41–2
   and anxiety 107
   and bullet lists 111
   and children's changing needs
      104
   and goal-setting 112
   helpful exercises for 111–15
   impact on our behaviour 105–6
   and journaling 112
   and labyrinth art 114–15, *115*
   of parenthood 101–4
   and positive focus 114
   and ritual and routine 113–14
   small 108–9, 116
   and visualisation 113
   what counts as 108
   what we need during 110–11
light
   blue 179
   red 179
limits, knowing your 210
list-making 111
load of parenting
   and gender inequality 78–82,
      83–8, 90, 92
   leaning to share 8, 75–99
   lightening the load 90–6
   and single parents 89–90
   and talking things through
      97–8
lockdowns 2, 99, 120–1, 187

Majethia, Niti 11
mantras 187
marketing 49
Martine, Christy Ann 100
Maslach, Christina 77
matrescence 102–3, 167
matriarchy 133–4
me-time 184–6

meal planning 83
medical needs 85
meditation 213
melatonin 179
memories, recording 88
menarche 113
menopause 104
mental abuse 142
mental health issues 21, 209
    see also anxiety; depression
mental load of parenting, leaning
    to share 8, 75–99
microbiome 180
mind
    conscious 16–17, 16, 29
    Freudian model of the 16–17,
        16
    preconscious 16, 16
    unconscious 16–17, 16
    see also subconscious
mindfulness 213
mistakes
    apologising for 201–3
    children's 201–2
    inability to accept other
        people's 46, 51
    inability to accept your own 46
    modelling acceptance of 54–5,
        201–3
    parenting 54–5, 200–3
    shaming children for 48, 49
modelling
    and the acceptance of mistakes
        54–5, 201–3
    failure of 19
    and handling big feelings 191–2
    and parental failure 55
    and self-kindness 189–90, 191–2
    and social comparison-making
        66
    and stress management 217
motherhood

and burnout 77
and 'good-enough' mothers
    53–4
transition to 102–3, 167
moving well 176, 180, 182–4, 214,
    216
Multidimensional Perfectionism
    Scale 50

nature, spending time in 176,
    186–8
'naughty' children 12–13
needs 9, 18, 172
    children's 104, 177–8
    dismissal of your 32
    and the fawn response 25
    needing to be liked by others 32
    of other people 13
    and self-kindness 192
    and sharing the load of
        parenting 75
    stepping on your 19, 25
    of working parents 158
neglect
    emotional 21
    physical 21
neurotransmitters 23
newborns 101–3
nirvana fallacy, the 45–6, 53, 59,
    62
no, learning to say 123–5, 129,
    131, 139–40, 164–5
noradrenaline 23
nurseries
    events 84
    liaison with 84
nutrient deficiency 177, 178, 180
nutrition 176–8, 176, 180

Obama, Michelle 173
other people
    and advice-giving 193–4

and comparison-making 72
expectations of 51–3
needing to be liked by **32**
needs 13
and trust issues 94–5
see also relationships; support
outdoor lifestyles 213, 216
outer self 5, 220
overscheduled children 127–8,
131
overwhelm 226
and the mental and physical
load of parenting 77, 79,
80, 89–90
and people-pleasing 139
and the sandwich generation
104
and single parents 89–90

pain 226
physical 64
social 64
staying calm through 208
parent influencers 67–9
parent–child dyad 200
parental attunement 200–1, 218
parental leave 163–4, 171
parental responsivity, good-
enough 54
parental tantrums 9, 198
and busy lifestyles 130
and the flight, fight, fawn and
freeze response 23
and the holler-and-heal cycle
200–1
and life transitions 109, 111
and the mental and physical
load of parenting 76,
79–80, 82, 96, 99
and present moment coping
199–219
and resting 186

self-blame regarding 190, 221
and self-care 182
and self-kindness 173
and sleep deprivation 182
parenthood
relentless nature 90–1, 178
transition to 103, 116, 167
parenting advice
giving 193–4
unsolicited 144–8
parenting beliefs, erroneous 37–8
parenting research **87**
parenting styles
authentic 8
authoritarian 25
disagreements regarding 149–50
patience 182
patrescence 103, 116, 167
patriarchy 134
peace–valuing 191
Peaceful Pentagon 173–98, *176*
checking 196–7
and eating well 176–8, *176*
and moving well *176*, 182–4
and resting well *176*, 184–6
and sleeping well *176*, 178–82
and spending time in nature
176, 186–8
people-pleasing 13, 25
and learning to say no 123
and relationships 139–40,
155–6
and self-worth 192
as trigger **32**
perfectionism 13, **33**
and life transitions 106
other-oriented 51
parenting 7–8, 42, 43–60
damaging nature 46–7
and 'good-enough' parenting
53–60
mechanisms of 47–50

perfectionism – *continued*
  and the nirvana fallacy 45–6,
    53, 59
  and overwhelm 89
  transgenerational effects 47
  self-oriented 50–1, 52, 60
  and social comparison-making
    65
  socially prescribed 51, 52, 60
  three main styles of 50–3
  transgenerational nature 47, 60
  and trust issues **34**
personal growth 66, 199
personhood, parental 38–9
perspective-taking 195
pet care **84**
physical abuse 21, 142
physical exercise *176*, 180, 182–4,
  214, 216
physical load of parenting,
  learning to share 8, 75–99
physical neglect 21
'picking your battles' 214
Pilates 183–4
pillows 180
play 214
  not having time for 79
  power of 122–3, 129
polyvagal theory 27–9, 38
popularity, need for **32**
Porges, Stephen 27–9
positive affirmations 57, 196,
  196–7
positive focus 114
positivity, toxic 65, 67
post-traumatic stress disorder
  (PTSD) 209
praise 13
prayer 213
preconscious mind 16, *16*
pregnancy loss 208
present, being 213, 225

present moment coping 9,
  199–219
  apologising in advance 203–4
  apologising to children 201–4
  during special circumstances
    207–11
  and emotional displacement
    206–7
  exercises 215–17
  and the path to calmer
    parenting 211–12
  and realistic expectations about
    children's behaviour 204–6
prioritization skills 93–4
prison inmates 21
privilege 5, 67, 89
procrastination 47, 51, 58, 60
psyche 12, 14, 93
PTSD *see* post-traumatic stress
  disorder
punctuality, effect of children on
  108–9
purpose, sense of 167

rage, sense of **32**
Raphael, Dana 102
re-parenting yourself 37
recognition
  asking for 95
  lack of **33**
reframing 57
regret 4, 44, 66
relationships 8, 132–56
  being happier alone 140
  and comparison-making 65
  difficult 21, 89, 133, 142–3
  ending 148, 156
  and the fawn response 25
  and making friends as an adult
    136–7, 155
  and the need for adult company
    8, 132, 168

positive 141–2
and separation 21, 89
supportive 132–56
that make you feel bad about
    your parenting skills 143–8
tips to improve 152–5
toxic 138, 148, 156
tribes 133–6, 138
and unpopularity 139–40
ups and downs 153–4
see also families
relaxation **34**
repression *see* emotional repression
research **87**
resentment 79, 80, 182, 208
resilience 6, 182
respect 12
    see also disrespect
responsivity, parental 54
resting well *176*, 184–6
rewards, extrinsic 48, 194–5
rituals 113–14
Rogers, Fred 199
role modelling *see* modelling
room temperature 179–80
routines, and life transitions
    113–14
rude children **32**
rupture–repair cycle (holler-and-
    heal cycle) 7, 9, 200–1, 207,
    211

safety, creating feelings of 28–9,
    38
Salmansohn, Karen 117
same-sex couples 78–9
sandwich generation 104
satiety 176
school
    events **84**
    liaison with **84**
    virtual 170

screaming, to relieve tension 216
screen time 179
self
    authentic 29–30, **32**, **34**, 38–9,
        195
    being honest with your 92
    comparison-making against
        (temporal comparison-
        making) 63, 66, 73
    finding out about yourself
        38–9
    imagining your future self 39
    inner 5, 220
    outer 5, 220
self-acceptance 41, 225
self-belief 13–14
self-blame 5, 52, 173–4, 190, 221
self-care 1, 9, 78, 120, 167–8, 174,
    188–9, 197
    see also self-kindness
self-compassion 110
self-criticism 13
self-empathy 14
self-employment, relentlessness of
    164–5
self-esteem 18
    and advertising 49
    children's 126, 189
    and comparison-making 64
    and perfectionism 44, 45, 51
    and seeing yourself through the
        eyes of others 195
    and self-kindness 189
self-forgiveness 71, 189, 190
self-improvement 66
self-judgmental attitudes 46
self-kindness 9, 14, 172, 173–98
    and eating well 176–8, *176*
    how to practice 190–7
    and letting go of childhood
        experiences 29, 31, 41
    not having time for 174–5

self-talk *see* inner dialogue/talk
self-worth 13, 47
  based on the opinions of
    others **32**
  and busy lifestyles 123
  and people pleasing 192
  and perfectionism 47, 51
  and popularity 139
  tidiness as measure of **33**
separation, parental 21, 89
Sesame Street (TV programme)
  219
setbacks 6, 221–2
sexual abuse 21
shame 4, 44, 48–9, 89
shinrin-yoku (forest bathing) 187
shouting 1, 3
siblings **33**, 49
single parents 89–90, 209
sleep deprivation 163–4, 181–2
sleep hygiene 179–81
sleep monitors 181
sleeping well *176*, 178–82
SNS *see* sympathetic nervous
  system
social comparison theory 66–7,
  73
social comparison-making 8, **33**,
  60, 61–74
  and acceptance 71
  between siblings **33**
  and correcting erroneous
    beliefs 71–2
  and embracing uniqueness 72
  how it can help us 63–4, 69–70
  and internal dialogue 70
  and life transitions 106
  management 69–72
  negative effects of 64–5
  people who bring out the worst
    in you 72
  and perfectionism 46

and social comparison theory
  66–7, 73
and social media 67–9, 73
social media 67–9, 73, 153
society, lack of support for
  parents 158
special occasions **85**
stay-at-home parents 157
  undervaluing of 49–50, 158
stereotypes, gender 78
stonewalling 148
stress 2, 217, 226
  avoidance 191
  bucket model of 19–20, *20*
  and busy lifestyles 118
  and comparison-making 69
  failure to resolve or regulate
    19
  and life transitions 100
  and the load of parenting 98
  and the need for headspace 96
  and over-busyness 130
  and parental burnout 77
  and perfectionism 45, 47
  and physical exercise 183
  recognition 214
  and sleep 181
  and spending time in nature
    187
  of working parents 162, 165–6
stress hormones 217
  see also adrenaline
stress responses
  fawn response 23–7, 46–7, 139
  fight response 23–9, 46–7
  flight response 23–7, **34**, 46–7,
    130
  freeze response 24, 27, 46, 47
  investigating/tuning into your
    30
subconscious 12–13, 145
  and change 101

and comparison-making 67
and perfectionism 48
substance abuse, parental 21
suicidal ideation 209
support
  and co-dependency 142
  from like-minded people 147–8
  lack of 52–3, 99, 135, 150–1,
    158
  and life transitions 110
  networks 39, 89, 99, 134, 216
  online 98, 147–8, 216
  and our relationships 132–56
survival mode 19
sympathetic nervous system
  (SNS) 23

taking on too much **34**, 190–1
'talking things through' 97–8,
  154
tantrums
  and life transitions 105
  see also parental tantrums
teachers 166
temper loss 5, 199–201, 220–1
  impact on your child 6–7, 222
  reflection on your 225
  what to do regarding 9
  see also parental tantrums
therapy 30, 39
  see also counselling
thinking, black-and-white 59
thought inventories 56
threat perception 19, 23–4, 26
tidiness, obsessive **33**
time out 17–18
tiredness 119, 143, 165, 182
  see also burnout; exhaustion
toxic positivity 65, 67
transgenerational effects 7, 47, 60
transport arrangements **87**
tribes 133–6, 140

triggers 7, 11–42, 182, 214, 223
  being aware of your 210
  examples 17–18
  exercises to deal with 31–9
  identifying key 31, **32–5**, 41
  investigating your 30
  and the load of parenting 89,
    96
Tronick, Ed 200
trust issues 13, **34**, 94–5
tunnel metaphor 211–12, 218

unconscious mind 16–17, *16*
uniqueness, embracing 72
unlovable, feeling 48

vagus nerve 27–8
validation
  reducing our sense of through
    comparison-making 65
  validation-seeking behaviour
    18, **32**, **33**, 139
van der Kolk, Bessel 14
verbal abuse 20
vicious circles 44
visualisation
  and calming places 215
  and labyrinth art 114
  and life transitions 113
Vitruvian Man 175
vulnerability
  embracing your 43
  fear of **34**

walking, barefoot 187
wellbeing 23, 45
wellness, emotional 187
Winnicott, Donald 53–4
Woodhouse, Susan S. 54
work–life balance 9, 157–70
  and childcare 162–3, 172
  flexibility in 170–1

work–life balance – *continued*
  and guilt 158, 159–62
  and lack of downtime 163
  positives of 161–2, 166–8
  and self-employment 164–5
  and sleep deprivation 163–4
  stress of 162
  and workplace support 171

working from home 121,
  169–70

yoga 183–4
YouGov polls 160

Zuckerberg, Mark 69